Religious Liberty

Other books in the Issues on Trial Series

Affirmative Action

Education

Euthanasia

Free Speech

Gun Control

Homosexuality

Immigration

Women's Rights

Religious Liberty

Sylvia Engdahl, Book Editor

GREENHAVEN PRESS
An imprint of Thomson Gale, a part of The Thomson Corporation

Detroit • New York • San Francisco • New Haven, Conn. • Waterville, Maine • London

Christine Nasso, *Publisher*
Elizabeth Des Chenes, *Managing Editor*

For more information, contact:
Greenhaven Press
27500 Drake Rd.
Farmington Hills, MI 48331-3535
Or you can visit our Internet site at http://www.gale.com

Articles in Greenhaven Press anthologies are often edited for length to meet page requirements. In addition, original titles of these works are changed to clearly present the main thesis and to explicitly indicate the author's opinion. Every effort is made to ensure that Greenhaven Press accurately reflects the original intent of the authors. Every effort has been made to trace the owners of copyrighted material.

LIBRARY OF CONGRESS CATALOGING-IN-PUBLICATION DATA

Religious Liberty / Sylvia Engdahl, book editor.
p. cm. -- (Issues on trial)
Includes bibliographical references and index.
ISBN-13: 978-0-7377-3855-1 (hardcover)
1. Freedom of Religion--United States--Cases--Juvenile literature. I. Engdahl, Sylvia, 1963-
KF4783.R45 2008
342.7308'52--dc22
2007027512

ISBN-10: 0-7377-3855-3 (hardcover)

Printed in the United States of America
10 9 8 7 6 5 4 3 2 1

Contents

Foreward 11

Introduction 14

Chapter 1: Balancing Religious Liberty Against School Attendance Laws

Case Overview: *Wisconsin v. Yoder* (1972) 20

1. The Court's Decision: The State's Interest in Universal Education Does Not Overrule the Fundamental Rights of Parents 22

   Warren Burger

   In *Wisconsin v. Yoder* the U.S. Supreme Court decided that parents cannot be required to send children to high school if it violates their religious beliefs to do so.

2. Dissenting Opinion: Children's Rights Should Be Considered as Well as Parents' Rights 32

   William O. Douglas

   Justice Douglas, dissenting in part from the Court's opinion, argues that it imposes the religious views of the parents on their children, potentially interfering with their own views.

3. The Question of Parental versus State Rights Is Still Not Settled 37

   Josh Chafetz

   A lawyer discusses why he believes the *Yoder* decision is not a satisfactory answer to the question of parental versus state rights.

4. The Ruling in Favor of the Amish Has Had a Lasting Impact on Religious and Home Schooling 48

   Shawn Francis Peters

   The author of a book about the *Yoder* case discusses the impact it has had on the issues of parental rights, home schooling, and state control of religious schools.

Chapter 2: Balancing Religious Liberty Against Prevailing Public Attitudes

Case Overview: *Church of Lukumi Babalu Aye v. City of Hialeah* (1993) **58**

1. The Court's Decision: Hialeah's Law Against Animal Sacrifice Was Intended to Suppress a Religion, Not to Protect Animals **61**

   Anthony Kennedy

   In *Church of Lukumi Babalu Aye v. City of Hialeah* the U.S. Supreme Court ruled that animal sacrifice during religious ceremonies cannot be prohibited where killing animals for other purposes is allowed.

2. Concurring Opinion: The Court Made the Right Judgment for the Wrong Reason **74**

   Harry Blackmun

   Justice Blackmun argues that although he agrees with the Court's decision, the value of religious freedom goes beyond mere antidiscrimination.

3. Minority Religions Are the Ones Most in Need of Constitutional Protection **78**

   Robert F. Drinan and Jennifer I. Huffman

   In anticipation of the U.S. Supreme Court's consideration of the *Hialeah* case, a law professor and a law student analyze the reasons why they believe the lower courts were wrong to uphold Hialeah's law against animal sacrifice.

4. Debate Centered on Whether Religious Discrimination or Public Health Was at Issue **87**

   David M. O'Brien

   A professor of political science describes one of the U.S. Supreme Court sessions in the *Hialeah* case, quoting from the oral arguments and the questions from the justices.

5. The Court's Opinion Reinforced the Principle of Equal Protection for All **99**
R. Ted Cruz
A lawyer argues that the U.S. Supreme Court was right to base its decision in the *Hialeah* case on the principle of equal protection, rather than on the question of whether there was a compelling state interest that would justify limitation of a religious practice.

Chapter 3: Balancing Religious Liberty Against Effective Management of Prisons

Case Overview: *Cutter et al. v. Wilkinson, Director, Ohio Department of Correction, et al.* (2005) **105**

1. The Court's Decision: There Is No Valid Reason to Deny the Practice of Non-Mainstream Religions in Prisons **108**
Ruth Bader Ginsburg
In *Cutter v. Wilkinson* the U.S. Supreme Court held that prison inmates of all religions must be allowed to practice them as long as it does not interfere with prison security.

2. Concurring Opinion: Accommodating Prisoners' Religious Practices Is Not Unconstitutional **117**
Clarence Thomas
Justice Thomas elaborates on the U.S. Supreme Court's opinion that providing for religious practices of prisoners does not constitute an unconstitutional establishment of religion.

3. The Rights of Prisoners Involve Principles That Guard Religious Freedom for Everyone **123**
Charles C. Haynes
Prior to the U.S. Supreme Court's consideration of *Cutter v. Wilkinson*, a scholar of the First Amendment argues that the outcome will have great implications for the future of religious freedom in America.

4. Prison Inmates Now Have the Right to Reasonable Religious Accommodations **127**

Jeremy Leaming

A spokesman for Americans United for Separation of Church and State explains restrictions prisoners have faced on the practice of their religions and discusses some of the issues the U.S. Supreme Court dealt with in *Cutter v. Wilkinson.*

5. The Supreme Court's Decision Was a Significant Victory for Minority Religions **136**

Dana D. Eilers

A retired attorney, herself a practicing pagan, explains the background of the *Cutter v. Wilkinson* case from the pagan standpoint and discusses what kind of impact the decision can be expected to have.

Chapter 4: Balancing Religious Liberty Against Prohibition of Hallucinogenic Drugs

Case Overview: *Gonzales, Attorney General, et al. v. O Centro Espirita Beneficiente Uniao do Vegetal, et al.* (2006) **143**

1. The Court's Decision: The Government Has Not Demonstrated a Compelling Reason for Allowing No Exceptions to the Controlled Substances Act **146**

John Roberts

In *Gonzales v. Uniao do Vegetal* the U.S. Supreme Court ruled that religious exemption from laws against drug use cannot be denied on the grounds of uniform law enforcement.

2. The Controlled Substances Act Should Be Enforced Without Exception, Even if this Limits Religious Freedom **156**

Paul D. Clement, et al.

U.S. government lawyers argue that all hallucinogenic drugs are unsafe and subject to abuse, and that therefore, use of them in religious services should not be exempt from the drug law.

3. There Is Now a Bright Future for Religious Liberty Cases 167

Kevin Eckstrom and Sarah Pulliam

Reporters for a Christian publication discuss the importance of the *Uniao do Vegetal* decision in ensuring the rights of all religions.

4. The Court Failed to Address a Critical Ambiguity in Its Prior Rulings 171

Michael C. Dorf

A law professor argues that because inconsistencies in previous religious liberty cases were not clarified by the ruling in *Uniao do Vegetal*, the issues they raise will probably return to the U.S. Supreme Court before long.

5. Separation of Church and State Is a Means of Implementing Religious Freedom 181

Richard Garnett

A law professor comments on what the *Uniao do Vegetal* decision reveals about the future of constitutional law and the balance between government interests and religious freedom.

Organizations to Contact 186

For Further Research 192

Index 198

Foreword

The U.S. courts have long served as a battleground for the most highly charged and contentious issues of the time. Divisive matters are often brought into the legal system by activists who feel strongly for their cause and demand an official resolution. Indeed, subjects that give rise to intense emotions or involve closely held religious or moral beliefs lay at the heart of the most polemical court rulings in history. One such case was *Brown v. Board of Education* (1954), which ended racial segregation in schools. Prior to *Brown*, the courts had held that blacks could be forced to use separate facilities as long as these facilities were equal to that of whites.

For years many groups had opposed segregation based on religious, moral, and legal grounds. Educators produced heartfelt testimony that segregated schooling greatly disadvantaged black children. They noted that in comparison to whites, blacks received a substandard education in deplorable conditions. Religious leaders such as Martin Luther King Jr. preached that the harsh treatment of blacks was immoral and unjust. Many involved in civil rights law, such as Thurgood Marshall, called for equal protection of all people under the law, as their study of the Constitution had indicated that segregation was illegal and un-American. Whatever their motivation for ending the practice, and despite the threats they received from segregationists, these ardent activists remained unwavering in their cause.

Those fighting against the integration of schools were mainly white southerners who did not believe that whites and blacks should intermingle. Blacks were subordinate to whites, they maintained, and society had to resist any attempt to break down strict color lines. Some white southerners charged that segregated schooling was *not* hindering blacks' education. For example, Virginia attorney general J. Lindsay Almond asserted, "With the help and the sympathy and the love and respect of the white people of the South, the colored man has risen under that educational process to a place of eminence and respect throughout the nation. It has served him well." So when the Supreme Court ruled against the segregationists in *Brown*, the South responded with vociferous cries of protest. Even government leaders criticized the decision. The governor of Arkansas, Orval Faubus, stated that he would not "be a party to any attempt to force acceptance of change to which the people are so overwhelmingly opposed." Indeed, resistance to integration was so great that when black students arrived at the formerly all-white Central High School in Arkansas, federal troops had to be dispatched to quell a threatening mob of protesters.

Nevertheless, the *Brown* decision was enforced and the South integrated its schools. In this instance, the Court, while not settling the issue to everyone's satisfaction, functioned as an instrument of progress by forcing a major social change. Historian David Halberstam observes that the *Brown* ruling "deprived segregationist practices of their moral legitimacy. . . . It was therefore perhaps the single most important moment of the decade, the moment that separated the old order from the new and helped create the tumultuous era just arriving." Considered one of the most important victories for civil rights, *Brown* paved the way for challenges to racial segregation in many areas, including on public buses and in restaurants.

In examining *Brown*, it becomes apparent that the courts play an influential role—and face an arduous challenge—in shaping the debate over emotionally charged social issues. Judges must balance competing interests, keeping in mind the high stakes and intense emotions on both sides. As exemplified by *Brown*, judicial decisions often upset the status quo and initiate significant changes in society. Greenhaven Press's Issues on Trial series captures the controversy surrounding influential court rulings and explores the social ramifications of such decisions from varying perspectives. Each anthology highlights one social issue—such as the death penalty, students' rights, or wartime civil liberties. Each volume then focuses on key historical and contemporary court cases that helped mold the issue as we know it today. The books include a compendium of primary sources—court rulings, dissents, and immediate reactions to the rulings—as well as secondary sources from experts in the field, people involved in the cases, legal analysts, and other commentators opining on the implications and legacy of the chosen cases. An annotated table of contents, an in-depth introduction, and prefaces that overview each case all provide context as readers delve into the topic at hand. To help students fully probe the subject, each volume contains book and periodical bibliographies, a comprehensive index, and a list of organizations to contact. With these features, the Issues on Trial series offers a well-rounded perspective on the courts' role in framing society's thorniest, most impassioned debates.

Introduction

In the United States, freedom of religion is a fundamental right. The First Amendment to the U.S. Constitution ensures that "Congress shall make no law respecting an establishment of religion, or prohibiting the free exercise thereof," and the Fourteenth Amendment extends this prohibition to state and local governments. Most Americans take the complete separation of church and state—which does not exist in countries that have official religions—for granted. They assume that, of course, everyone is free to follow his or her own religion without government interference.

Religious freedom, however, is not quite that simple. What happens when the beliefs of a minority religious group conflict with other principles that Americans consider important? And what happens when people who do not have any religion object to the expression of majority religious beliefs by tax-supported institutions or on public property? If these were easy questions to answer, it would not be necessary for the Supreme Court of the United States, the justices (judges) of which are among the finest and most experienced legal scholars in the nation, to spend time considering them. As it is, many religious liberty cases come before the Court and its members do not always agree about them.

There are two distinct types of court cases that arise. One type involves the *establishment clause* of the First Amendment, which says laws cannot be made "respecting an establishment of religion" (in other words, that establish religion as an official policy of the government). Issues such as whether prayer may be allowed in public schools are establishment cases because allowing prayer in tax-supported schools would imply that the government officially endorses prayer. The second type of case involves the *free exercise clause* (which says that the "free exercise" of religion cannot be prohibited). All of the cases presented in this book are free exercise cases.

It may seem that free exercise cases, which usually involve small minorities, would affect only the members of those minorities, and that nobody else would be concerned with them apart from wanting to defend minority rights. But in fact, the impact of such cases is far-reaching and touches far more people than those directly affected by the Court's ruling. The reason for this is that when the Supreme Court (or any court) issues an opinion about a case, every statement in that opinion sets a precedent that can be cited in future cases. Court opinions are full of quotations from previous cases, and this is not because judges could not express the same ideas just as well in their own words—it is because precedents are what legal decisions are based on. If a precedent is set by the wording of a judge's opinion in a case involving just a few people, it may later support or even determine decisions that involve many people. Judges are free to disregard precedents, but to do so requires stronger justification than to follow them. Therefore, the outcome of any court case that concerns religious liberty is important to everyone.

The free exercise clause of the First Amendment states so clearly that every person has the right to free exercise of religion that there appears to be no room for argument. When this right is called into question, it is a matter of balancing one principle against another of equal or greater importance. For example, if there were a religion in America that involved human sacrifice, that form of free exercise would certainly not be allowed. Obviously, then, the words of the Constitution cannot be interpreted literally, without any exceptions. The courts have to decide what exceptions should be permitted, and most of the time, religious freedom overrides the other considerations that lead exceptions to be sought.

There is, however, one thing that Americans commonly view as more important than religious liberty, and that is the health of children. Some religions reject standard medical treatment; their members believe that healing by means of prayer or other spiritual practices is more effective, or that their children's spiritual welfare matters more than their physical health. Recognizing this, many states have laws that provide religious exemptions to medical care that parents would otherwise be required to obtain for their children. But there is growing opposition to these laws. "The religious exemption laws are a rare example of discrimination de jure: laws that deprive one group of children of protections afforded to others," said Rita Swan, who is president of the organization Children's Healthcare Is a Legal Duty (CHILD).

Swan and many others view failure to take sick children to a doctor as a form of child abuse. Yet members of religions who reject medical care do not intend to harm their children—they sincerely believe that they will be helped more by faith and that medical attention would be harmful to them. People on both sides of the issue want to do the right thing, and there is an irreconcilable conflict between them.

Mentally competent adults now have the right, confirmed by the Supreme Court, to reject medical treatment for any reason whatsoever, religious or otherwise. But whether they have any legal right to reject it for their children is less clear. When children who have not received medical care die, as sometimes happens, the parents are often held criminally liable even if the practice of their religion required them to act as they did; in most states religious exemptions to child neglect laws are not a defense against charges of manslaughter or murder. The Supreme Court has not reviewed a case of this kind, but the precedents it set in other cases involving parental rights are often cited by the lower courts.

One of these precedents comes from the famous 1944 case *Prince v. Commonwealth of Massachusetts*. In this case, the Court upheld the conviction of Sarah Prince for violating child labor laws by allowing her nine-year-old ward to help her distribute religious literature on the street. It had nothing to do with denial of medical care. Nevertheless, in delivering the opinion of the Court, Justice Wiley Rutledge discussed parental rights in general; he wrote, "The right to practice religion freely does not include liberty to expose the community or the child to communicable disease or the latter to ill health or death. . . . Parents may be free to become martyrs themselves. But it does not follow they are free, in identical circumstances, to make martyrs of their children before they have reached the age of full and legal discretion and can make that choice for themselves."

An example of a case in which this precedent proved decisive is *Barnhart v. Commonwealth of Pennsylvania*, which was heard on appeal by the Superior Court of Pennsylvania in 1985. William and Linda Barnhart, members of the Faith Tabernacle Church, were convicted of manslaughter after their two-year-old son died of cancer because they had relied on faith healing rather than modern medical care. The judge wrote, "Our decision today directly penalizes appellants' exercise of their religious beliefs. Appellants ask how we can hold them criminally liable for putting their faith in God. No easy answer attends. . . . The guarantee of freedom of religion is intended to secure the rights of the individual as against the state. Underlying the guarantee is a principle of neutrality, a belief that religion is 'not within the cognizance of civil government.' . . . However nice the distinction in theory, as the case at bar attests it sometimes fails in practice." He then went on to quote the above passages from the *Prince* case, along with several other legal precedents, and upheld the conviction on the grounds that the child had not been old enough to speak on his own behalf.

Some people argue that modern medicine, too, involves beliefs held on faith; that it cannot not always cure diseases such as cancer; and that it should not be given legal precedence over the beliefs of individual citizens merely because its premises are accepted by the majority. Moreover, as C.D. Herrera has written in the *Journal of Church and State*, "The state's close involvement with medical research, education and certification prevents it from being a disinterested spectator . . . [its] close involvement with medicine dictates a particular interpretation of what is in the child's best interests." And yet, someone has to make decisions that children cannot make for themselves. Should it be the government or the parents, when both are biased? This is a larger issue than the question of what treatment they should receive when ill. As far as religious liberty is concerned, children generally have no choice about what religion will be "theirs" in the first place—the government cannot force it on them, but their parents can.

The question of children's religious beliefs was considered in the case of *Wisconsin v. Yoder* (1972), which is one of those presented in this book and which was also cited by the judge in *Barnhart v. Pennsylvania*. In *Yoder*, the Supreme Court ruled that the parents have the right to determine, on religious grounds, the education of their teenage children. In a dissenting opinion, Justice William O. Douglas maintained that children's own rights should also be considered because "children are 'persons' within the meaning of the Bill of Rights." But where children's welfare is at stake, this does not solve the problem of choosing between free exercise of religion and the majority opinion of society. As in every other situation where a dispute reaches the courts, it can be dealt with only case by case, by judges doing their best to balance conflicting values.

Chapter 1

Balancing Religious Liberty Against School Attendance Laws

Chapter Preface

Case Overview: *Wisconsin v. Yoder* (1972)

In 1968 three Amish farmers were charged with violating the State of Wisconsin's compulsory school attendance law by refusing to send their teenage children to high school. The Old Order Amish are quiet, hardworking people who live by the rules of their religion in communities isolated from the modern world. They dress modestly and speak a German dialect known as Pennsylvania Dutch. They use horse-drawn buggies because they do not believe in owning cars or other modern equipment, and they do not have television or even telephones in their homes.

Amish children attend school through the eighth grade to acquire basic skills such as reading and arithmetic, and to learn English for interacting with non-Amish people when necessary. In some areas they have their own elementary schools; in others they go to public ones. But it is against their religious beliefs to attend high school because the subjects taught there are designed to prepare young people for modern life, and therefore include many ideas that are contrary to the Amish religion—ideas by which parents do not want their children to be influenced. They do not want them to participate in school activities or competitive sports. Furthermore, they feel that during adolescence their children should spend their time learning the work skills and attitudes they will need as adults in their own communities.

The Amish do not believe in going to court to settle disputes, and their religion forbids them to hire lawyers. Nevertheless, though they were reluctant to do so, the farmers—Jonas Yoder, Wallace Miller, and Adin Yutzy—eventually allowed themselves to be represented by an organization called the National Committee for Amish Religious Freedom

(NCARF), whose members are not Amish but who wish to defend the principle of religious liberty. After trial by a county court the three men were convicted, and their conviction was upheld on appeal. The Wisconsin Supreme Court then agreed to hear the case. That court reversed the decision of the lower court, ruling that compulsory high school attendance would infringe on the religious freedom of the Amish and was therefore unconstitutional.

The State of Wisconsin would not allow the case to drop; its attorney general petitioned the U.S. Supreme Court for review on grounds that compulsory education laws throughout the nation had been threatened by its outcome. In its case to the Supreme Court, the state maintained, among other arguments, that education is necessary to prepare citizens to participate in democracy and to become self-reliant members of society. The NCARF attorney argued that this was not a sufficient reason to deny religious freedom by requiring attendance at public high schools, and that the education Amish teenagers received at home did, in fact, prepare them for adult life in the communities where they lived. The Supreme Court agreed. In its 1972 decision that high school attendance could not be required of the Amish, it emphasized that their beliefs were a part of their religion, not merely a philosophical preference, and that Amish people were exceptionally good citizens with a long history of self-reliance who never caused trouble in society.

In the years following the *Wisconsin v. Yoder* case, the precedent it set has had a major impact on the issues of parental rights, home schooling, and state regulation of religious schools. Its impact on religious liberty in general has been less durable, for the basis of the ruling—that freedom to practice one's religion can be overridden by a law only if there is a compelling governmental interest in universal enforcement of it—was overturned later by *Employment Division v. Smith* (1990). Nevertheless, it is considered a landmark case for freedom of religion.

"The record in this case abundantly supports the claim that the traditional way of life of the Amish is not merely a matter of personal preference, but one of deep religious conviction."

The Court's Decision: The State's Interest in Universal Education Does Not Overrule the Fundamental Rights of Parents

Warren Burger

Warren Burger was the chief justice of the Supreme Court at the time this case was decided. The following viewpoint is an excerpt from his opinion, representing the majority of the Court. It describes the objection of the Amish to sending their children to high school and the Court's conclusion that it is based on their religious beliefs, not simply on philosophy. Evidence that the home education provided for Amish teenagers prepares them for life in their community is also summarized. Chief Justice Burger explains why the Court decided that these facts override the State of Wisconsin's claim that high school attendance should be compulsory for everyone. Finally, he states that the question of a potential conflict between the parents' wishes and those of their children is not relevant to the case because no evidence was presented suggesting that any of them want to go to high school, and because non-Amish parents also make educational decisions for their teenage children.

Warren Burger, majority opinion, *Wisconsin v. Yoder et al.*, U.S. Supreme Court, May 15, 1972.

Respondents Jonas Yoder and Wallace Miller are members of the Old Order Amish religion, and respondent Adin Yutzy is a member of the Conservative Amish Mennonite Church. They and their families are residents of Green County, Wisconsin. Wisconsin's compulsory school-attendance law required them to cause their children to attend public or private school until reaching age 16 but the respondents declined to send their children, ages 14 and 15, to public school after they completed the eighth grade. The children were not enrolled in any private school, or within any recognized exception to the compulsory-attendance law, and they are conceded to be subject to the Wisconsin statute.

On complaint of the school district administrator for the public schools, respondents were charged, tried, and convicted of violating the compulsory-attendance law in Green County Court and were fined the sum of $5 each. Respondents defended on the ground that the application of the compulsory-attendance law violated their rights under the First and Fourteenth Amendments. The trial testimony showed that respondents believed, in accordance with the tenets of Old Order Amish communities generally, that their children's attendance at high school, public or private, was contrary to the Amish religion and way of life. They believed that by sending their children to high school, they would not only expose themselves to the danger of the censure of the church community, but, as found by the county court, also endanger their own salvation and that of their children. The State stipulated that respondents' religious beliefs were sincere. . . .

The Amish Objection to High School

Old Order Amish communities today are characterized by a fundamental belief that salvation requires life in a church community separate and apart from the world and worldly influence. This concept of life aloof from the world and its values is central to their faith.

A related feature of Old Order Amish communities is their devotion to a life in harmony with nature and the soil, as exemplified by the simple life of the early Christian era that continued in America during much of our early national life. Amish beliefs require members of the community to make their living by farming or closely related activities. . . .

Amish objection to formal education beyond the eighth grade is firmly grounded in these central religious concepts. They object to the high school, and higher education generally, because the values they teach are in marked variance with Amish values and the Amish way of life; they view secondary school education as an impermissible exposure of their children to a "worldly" influence in conflict with their beliefs. The high school tends to emphasize intellectual and scientific accomplishments, self-distinction, competitiveness, worldly success, and social life with other students. Amish society emphasizes informal learning-through-doing; a life of "goodness," rather than a life of intellect; wisdom, rather than technical knowledge; community welfare, rather than competition; and separation from, rather than integration with, contemporary worldly society.

Formal high school education beyond the eighth grade is contrary to Amish beliefs, not only because it places Amish children in an environment hostile to Amish beliefs with increasing emphasis on competition in class work and sports and with pressure to conform to the styles, manners, and ways of the peer group, but also because it takes them away from their community, physically and emotionally, during the crucial and formative adolescent period of life. . . .

The Amish do not object to elementary education through the first eight grades as a general proposition because they agree that their children must have basic skills in the "three R's" in order to read the Bible, to be good farmers and citizens, and to be able to deal with non-Amish people when necessary in the course of daily affairs. They view such a basic education as acceptable because it does not significantly expose their children to worldly values or interfere with their development in the Amish community during the crucial adolescent period. While Amish accept compulsory elementary education generally, wherever possible they have established their own elementary schools in many respects like the small local schools of the past. . . .

Their Objection Is Based on Religion, Not Philosophy

A State's interest in universal education, however highly we rank it, is not totally free from a balancing process when it impinges on fundamental rights and interests, such as those specifically protected by the Free Exercise Clause of the First Amendment, and the traditional interest of parents with respect to the religious upbringing of their children so long as they, in the words of *Pierce* [*v. Society of Sisters*, a 1925 case concerning mandatory attendance in public schools] "prepare them for additional obligations."

It follows that in order for Wisconsin to compel school attendance beyond the eighth grade against a claim that such attendance interferes with the practice of a legitimate religious belief, it must appear either that the State does not deny the free exercise of religious belief by its requirement, or that there is a state interest of sufficient magnitude to override the interest claiming protection under the Free Exercise Clause. Long before there was general acknowledgment of the need for universal formal education, the Religion Clauses had specifically and firmly fixed the right to free exercise of religious beliefs, and buttressing this fundamental right was an equally firm, even if less explicit, prohibition against the establishment of any religion by government. The values underlying these two provisions relating to religion have been zealously protected, sometimes even at the expense of other interests of admittedly high social importance. . . .

We must be careful to determine whether the Amish religious faith and their mode of life are, as they claim, inseparable and interdependent. A way of life, however virtuous and admirable, may not be interposed as a barrier to reasonable state regulation of education if it is based on purely secular considerations; to have the protection of the Religion Clauses, the claims must be rooted in religious belief. Although a determination of what is a "religious" belief or practice entitled to constitutional protection may present a most delicate question, the very concept of ordered liberty precludes allowing every person to make his own standards on matters of conduct in which society as a whole has important interests. Thus, if the Amish asserted their claims because of their subjective evaluation and rejection of the contemporary secular values accepted by the majority, much as [nineteenth-century American writer Henry David] Thoreau rejected the social values of his time and isolated himself at Walden Pond, their claims would not rest on a religious basis. Thoreau's choice was philosophical and personal rather than religious, and such belief does not rise to the demands of the Religion Clauses.

Giving no weight to such secular considerations, however, we see that the record in this case abundantly supports the claim that the traditional way of life of the Amish is not merely a matter of personal preference but one of deep religious conviction, shared by an organized group, and intimately related to daily living. . . .

The impact of the compulsory-attendance law on respondents' practice of the Amish religion is not only severe, but inescapable, for the Wisconsin law affirmatively compels them, under threat of criminal sanction, to perform acts undeniably at odds with fundamental tenets of their religious beliefs. Nor is the impact of the compulsory-attendance law confined to grave interference with important Amish religious tenets from a subjective point of view. It carries with it precisely the kind of objective danger to the free exercise of religion that the First Amendment was designed to prevent. As the record shows, compulsory school attendance to age 16 for Amish children carries with it a very real threat of undermining the Amish community and religious practice as they exist today; they must either abandon belief and be assimilated into society at large, or be forced to migrate to some other and more tolerant region. . . .

Wisconsin concedes that under the Religion Clauses religious beliefs are absolutely free from the State's control, but it argues that "actions," even though religiously grounded, are outside the protection of the First Amendment. But our decisions have rejected the idea that religiously grounded conduct is always outside the protection of the Free Exercise Clause. It is true that activities of individuals, even when religiously based, are often subject to regulation by the States in the exercise of their undoubted power to promote the health, safety, and general welfare, or the Federal Government in the exercise of its delegated powers.

But to agree that religiously grounded conduct must often be subject to the broad police power of the State is not to deny that there are areas of conduct protected by the Free Exercise Clause of the First Amendment and thus beyond the power of the State to control, even under regulations of general applicability. . . . This case, therefore, does not become easier because respondents were convicted for their "actions" in refusing to send their children to the public high school; in this context belief and action cannot be neatly confined in logic-tight compartments.

Nor can this case be disposed of on the grounds that Wisconsin's requirement for school attendance to age 16 applies uniformly to all citizens of the State and does not, on its face, discriminate against religions or a particular religion, or that it is motivated by legitimate secular concerns. A regulation neutral on its face may, in its application, nonetheless offend the constitutional requirement for governmental neutrality if it unduly burdens the free exercise of religion. . . .

Amish Education Prepares Adolescents for Life

We turn, then, to the State's broader contention that its interest in its system of compulsory education is so compelling that even the established religious practices of the Amish must give way. Where fundamental claims of religious freedom are at stake, however, we cannot accept such a sweeping claim. . . .

The State advances two primary arguments in support of its system of compulsory education. It notes, as Thomas Jefferson pointed out early in our history, that some degree of education is necessary to prepare citizens to participate effectively and intelligently in our open political system if we are to preserve freedom and independence. Further, education prepares individuals to be self-reliant and self-sufficient participants in society. We accept these propositions.

However, the evidence adduced by the Amish in this case is persuasively to the effect that an additional one or two years of formal high school for Amish children in place of their long-established program of informal vocational education would do little to serve those interests. Respondents' experts testified at trial, without challenge, that the value of all education must be assessed in terms of its capacity to prepare the child for life. It is one thing to say that compulsory education for a year or two beyond the eighth grade may be necessary when its goal is the preparation of the child for life in modern society as the majority live, but it is quite another if the goal of education be viewed as the preparation of the child for life in the separated agrarian community that is the keystone of the Amish faith.

The State attacks respondents' position as one fostering "ignorance" from which the child must be protected by the State. No one can question the State's duty to protect children from ignorance but this argument does not square with the facts disclosed in the record. Whatever their idiosyncrasies as seen by the majority, this record strongly shows that the Amish community has been a highly successful social unit within our society, even if apart from the conventional "mainstream." Its members are productive and very law-abiding members of society. . . .

It is neither fair nor correct to suggest that the Amish are opposed to education beyond the eighth grade level. What this record shows is that they are opposed to conventional formal education of the type provided by a certified high school because it comes at the child's crucial adolescent period of religious development. Dr. Donald Erickson, for example, testified that their system of learning-by-doing was an "ideal system" of education in terms of preparing Amish children for life as adults in the Amish community, and that "I would be inclined to say they do a better job in this than most of the rest of us do." . . .

The State, however, supports its interest in providing an additional one or two years of compulsory high school education to Amish children because of the possibility that some such children will choose to leave the Amish community, and that if this occurs they will be ill-equipped for life. The State argues that if Amish children leave their church they should not be in the position of making their way in the world without the education available in the one or two additional years the State requires. However, on this record, that argument is highly speculative. There is no specific evidence of the loss of Amish adherents by attrition, nor is there any showing that upon leaving the Amish community Amish children, with their practical agricultural training and habits of industry and self-reliance, would become burdens on society because of educational short-comings. . . .

When Thomas Jefferson emphasized the need for education as a bulwark of a free people against tyranny, there is nothing to indicate he had in mind compulsory education through any fixed age beyond a basic education. Indeed, the Amish communities singularly parallel and reflect many of the virtues of Jefferson's ideal of the "sturdy yeoman" who would form the basis of what he considered as the ideal of a democratic society. Even their idiosyncratic separateness exemplifies the diversity we profess to admire and encourage. . . .

Conflict Between Parents' and Children's Wishes Is Not an Issue

Finally, the State . . . argues that a decision exempting Amish children from the State's requirement fails to recognize the substantive right of the Amish child to a secondary education, and fails to give due regard to the power of the State as *parens patriae* [guardian of all minors] to extend the benefit of secondary education to children regardless of the wishes of their parents. . . .

Contrary to the suggestion of the dissenting opinion of Mr. Justice Douglas, our holding today in no degree depends on the assertion of the religious interest of the child as contrasted with that of the parents. It is the parents who are subject to prosecution here for failing to cause their children to attend school, and it is their right of free exercise, not that of their children, that must determine Wisconsin's power to impose criminal penalties on the parent. The dissent argues that a child who expresses a desire to attend public high school in conflict with the wishes of his parents should not be prevented from doing so. There is no reason for the Court to consider that point since it is not an issue in the case. The children are not parties to this litigation. The State has at no point tried this case on the theory that respondents were preventing their children from attending school against their expressed desires, and indeed the record is to the contrary. The State's position from the outset has been that it is empowered to apply its compulsory-attendance law to Amish parents in the same manner as to other parents—that is, without regard to the wishes of the child. That is the claim we reject today.

Our holding in no way determines the proper resolution of possible competing interests of parents, children, and the State in an appropriate state court proceeding in which the power of the State is asserted on the theory that Amish parents are preventing their minor children from attending high school despite their expressed desires to the contrary. . . .

The State's argument proceeds without reliance on any actual conflict between the wishes of parents and children. It appears to rest on the potential that exemption of Amish parents from the requirements of the compulsory-education law might allow some parents to act contrary to the best interests of their children by foreclosing their opportunity to make an intelligent choice between the Amish way of life and that of the outside world. The same argument could, of course, be made with respect to all church schools short of college. There is nothing in the record or in the ordinary course of human experience to suggest that non-Amish parents generally consult with children of ages 14–16 if they are placed in a church school of the parents' faith. . . .

The history and culture of Western civilization reflect a strong tradition of parental concern for the nurture and upbringing of their children. This primary role of the parents in the upbringing of their children is now established beyond debate as an enduring American tradition.

"It is the student's judgment, not his parents', that is essential if we are to give full meaning to what we have said about . . . the right of students to be masters of their own destiny."

Dissenting Opinion: Children's Rights Should Be Considered as Well as Parents' Rights

William O. Douglas

William O. Douglas was a justice of the U.S. Supreme Court. The following viewpoint is the portion of his opinion in the Wisconsin v. Yoder *case that deals with the rights of teenage students as distinguished from the rights of their parents. The Court ruled that Amish parents cannot be forced to send their children to high school because it is against their religious beliefs to do so. Although Justice Douglas agreed with the majority that religious exceptions to the school attendance law should be made, he argues in his opinion that the beliefs of the children themselves should have been considered. In many past cases, he states, the Court recognized that teenage students are "persons" within the meaning of the Bill of Rights. To impose the religious views of their parents concerning education on them could imperil their future, as they might wish to choose occupations not compatible with the Amish way of life. Only one of the children involved in the case was given opportunity to testify that she herself was opposed to high school education. Therefore, Justice Douglas dissented from the majority decision with respect to the others.*

William O. Douglas, dissenting opinion, *Wisconsin v. Yoder et al.*, U.S. Supreme Court, May 15, 1972.

I agree with the Court that the religious scruples of the Amish are opposed to the education of their children beyond the grade schools, yet I disagree with the Court's conclusion that the matter is within the dispensation of parents alone. The Court's analysis assumes that the only interests at stake in the case are those of the Amish parents on the one hand, and those of the State on the other. The difficulty with this approach is that, despite the Court's claim, the parents are seeking to vindicate not only their own free exercise claims, but also those of their high-school-age children.

It is argued that the right of the Amish children to religious freedom is not presented by the facts of the case, as the issue before the Court involves only the Amish parents' religious freedom to defy a state criminal statute imposing upon them an affirmative duty to cause their children to attend high school.

First, respondents' motion to dismiss in the trial court expressly asserts, not only the religious liberty of the adults, but also that of the children, as a defense to the prosecutions. It is, of course, beyond question that the parents have standing as defendants in a criminal prosecution to assert the religious interests of their children as a defense. Although the lower courts and a majority of this Court assume an identity of interest between parent and child, it is clear that they have treated the religious interest of the child as a factor in the analysis.

Second, it is essential to reach the question to decide the case, not only because the question was squarely raised in the motion to dismiss, but also because no analysis of religious-liberty claims can take place in a vacuum. If the parents in this case are allowed a religious exemption, the inevitable effect is to impose the parents' notions of religious duty upon their children. Where the child is mature enough to express potentially conflicting desires, it would be an invasion of the child's rights to permit such an imposition without canvassing his views. It is an imposition resulting from this very litigation. As the child has no other effective forum, it is in this litigation that his rights should be considered. And, if an Amish child desires to attend high school, and is mature enough to have that desire respected, the State may well be able to override the parents' religiously motivated objections.

Religion is an individual experience. It is not necessary, nor even appropriate, for every Amish child to express his views on the subject in a prosecution of a single adult. Crucial, however, are the views of the child whose parent is the subject of the suit. Frieda Yoder has in fact testified that her own religious views are opposed to high-school education. I therefore join the judgment of the Court as to respondent Jonas Yoder. But Frieda Yoder's views may not be those of Vernon Yutzy or Barbara Miller. I must dissent, therefore, as to respondents Adin Yutzy and Wallace Miller as their motion to dismiss also raised the question of their children's religious liberty.

The Children's Views Should Be Heard

This issue has never been squarely presented before today. Our opinions are full of talk about the power of the parents over the child's education. And we have in the past analyzed similar conflicts between parent and State with little regard for the views of the child. Recent cases, however, have clearly held that the children themselves have constitutionally protectible interests.

These children are "persons" within the meaning of the Bill of Rights. We have so held over and over again. . . .

In *Tinker v. Des Moines School District*, we dealt with 13-year-old, 15-year-old, and 16-year-old students who wore armbands to public schools and were disciplined for doing so. We gave them relief, saying that their First Amendment rights had been abridged.

> Students in school as well as out of school are "persons" under our Constitution. They are possessed of fundamental

rights which the State must respect, just as they themselves must respect their obligations to the State.

In *Board of Education v. Barnette*, we held that schoolchildren, whose religious beliefs collided with a school rule requiring them to salute the flag, could not be required to do so. While the sanction included expulsion of the students and prosecution of the parents, the vice of the regime was its interference with the child's free exercise of religion. We said: "Here . . . we are dealing with a compulsion of students to declare a belief." In emphasizing the important and delicate task of boards of education we said:

> That they are educating the young for citizenship is reason for scrupulous protection of Constitutional freedoms of the individual, if we are not to strangle the free mind at its source and teach youth to discount important principles of our government as mere platitudes.

On this important and vital matter of education, I think the children should be entitled to be heard. While the parents, absent dissent, normally speak for the entire family, the education of the child is a matter on which the child will often have decided views. He may want to be a pianist or an astronaut or an oceanographer. To do so he will have to break from the Amish tradition.

It is the future of the student, not the future of the parents, that is imperiled by today's decision. If a parent keeps his child out of school beyond the grade school, then the child will be forever barred from entry into the new and amazing world of diversity that we have today. The child may decide that that is the preferred course, or he may rebel. It is the student's judgment, not his parents', that is essential if we are to give full meaning to what we have said about the Bill of Rights and of the right of students to be masters of their own destiny. If he is harnessed to the Amish way of life by those in authority over him and if his education is truncated, his entire life may be stunted and deformed. The child, therefore, should be given an opportunity to be heard before the State gives the exemption which we honor today.

The views of the two children in question were not canvassed by the Wisconsin courts. The matter should be explicitly reserved so that new hearings can be held on remand of the case.

> *"The* Yoder *problem is still very much with us. . . . It is a difficult problem, necessitating an examination of some of the deepest principles underpinning our collective life."*

The Question of Parental Versus State Rights Is Still Not Settled

Josh Chafetz

Josh Chafetz is a student at Yale Law School, where he is an editor for the Yale Law & Policy Review *and the* Yale Law Journal. *He has written for many major publications and is the author of a book,* Democracy's Privileged Few. *In the following viewpoint he maintains that the underlying question of when, if ever, parents have a religious freedom-based claim to exempt their children from a state-mandated educational requirement was not settled by the U.S. Supreme Court's decision in the* Yoder *case. He points out that the issue is important today because of current debate over what should be taught in the public schools and how much control parents should have over their children's education. This excerpt from Chafetz's article includes his summary of his objections to various positions that agree or disagree with the* Yoder *decision, as well as arguments for his belief that such decisions should be made democratically rather than by the courts.*

Josh Chafetz, "Social Reproduction and Religious Reproduction: A Democratic-Communitarian Analysis of the *Yoder* Problem," *WM. & MARY BILL RTS. J. 263 (2006).*

Wisconsin v. Yoder presented the Court with a sharp clash between the state's interest in social reproduction through education—that is, society's interest in using the educational system to perpetuate its collective way of life among the next generation—and the parents' interest in religious reproduction—that is, their interest in passing their religious beliefs on to their children. This Article will take up the challenge of that clash. I shall refer throughout to the question of when, if ever, parents have a religious freedom-based claim to exempt their children from part or all of a state-mandated educational requirement as "the *Yoder* question," but the inquiry is not focused on the facts of the case itself. Rather, I shall engage with the competing theories put forward by scholars and judges who believe in a broad right of religious reproduction, trumping the state's interest in social reproduction ("*Yoder* supporters") and scholars and judges who believe that the interest in social reproduction should trump contrary claims by insular religious groups ("*Yoder* opponents"). I will suggest that each of the major competing theories is fundamentally flawed, and I will offer an alternative analysis based on communitarian [a type of social organization] and democratic values.

It is especially important that we continue to think through these issues because *Yoder* by no means settled the *Yoder* question. As debates continue to rage about issues like the teaching of evolution, creationism, or intelligent design in public schools, it remains clear that our society continues to struggle with the proper line between societal and parental control over education. It should also be noted that this is an area of constitutional law in which originalist methodologies give scant guidance—education was not seen as a state function in the early republic. Prior to the passage of the Fourteenth Amendment, the religion clauses of the First Amendment applied only to the federal government, and education was certainly not seen as a federal function. Our analysis will thus have to rely on other interpretive methodologies, including a consideration of the political values underlying our conceptions of religious freedom and education.

Decisions Should Be Made Democratically

The democratic-communitarian analysis of the *Yoder* problem offered in this Article begins with the communitarian intuition that social subjects are constituted by multiple sources of value—everything from low-level value sources like families and churches to higher-level sources like political parties and nations—and that a rich diversity of value sources is important and worth fostering. Totalitarianism, however, can result when high-level value sources (i.e., those value sources further away from the individual—for example, political parties, states, nations, and the international community) become too thick and squeeze out the possibility of diversity among individual citizens. A proper communitarian theory will therefore take into account the various competences of different social institutions to promote the diversity of values that are constitutive of our subjectivity, while simultaneously bearing in mind that these value sources ought to be thickest at the lowest levels. This analysis will conclude that schools are uniquely well situated to promote those values held at the society-wide level. This will combine with the democratic intuition that, in a democratic society, decisions about the inculcation of social values can only legitimately be made by democratic means. The conclusion will be that parents and courts are unjustified in interfering with social reproduction through schooling.

However, the democratic-communitarian analysis produces a second, equally important conclusion. When making democratic decisions, the conscientious citizen and legislator are bound to resist totalitarian tendencies by imposing the minimum restraints necessary to ensure the transmission of important communal values at each level. In other words, voters should very seriously consider enacting the kinds of exemptions sought by Jonas Yoder and his co-defendants, and they should decide not to enact those exemptions only if they come to the conclusion that the exemptions will interfere with instruction necessary for the education of democratic citizens.

This democratic-communitarian theory is best explored against the background of the competing analyses of the *Yoder* problem heretofore offered by scholars. These competing analyses have raised problems and concerns that must be addressed by any new entrant into the field. This Article thus begins by responding to each of the four main lines of existing scholarship on the *Yoder* question.

. . . I [shall] examine the case from liberal neutrality against *Yoder* and the case from liberal neutrality in favor of *Yoder*. I conclude that each of these positions is inadequate. The *Yoder* opponent cannot escape the fact that there is no value-neutral curriculum, and the *Yoder* supporter cannot abide the logical consequences of his position—that *all* laws, not merely educational ones, should be neutral among competing conceptions of the good. The arguments from liberal neutrality are inadequate because they both import other, non-neutral values *sub rosa* [covertly] in an attempt to make it appear that neutral reflection leads to their preferred outcome.

. . . I [will then] consider the parentalist case in favor of *Yoder*. I reject the parentalist case as incomplete because it fails to consider the complex web of social relations that constitutes a child's value set. It is only by misunderstanding the complexity of social relations that parentalist theorists can conclude that the parents are the only legitimate source of values for the child or that compulsory public schooling will stifle social dissent.

. . . [Next] I turn to the republican case against *Yoder*. [This refers to believers in a republican form of government, not to the Republican Party.] I conclude that the republican argument creates unjustified impositions on democratic decision-making. What it masks as curricular conditions necessary for democracy are, in fact, simply the entrenchment of the republican's own curricular preferences. . . .

I turn [lastly] . . . to an explication of the democratic-communitarian alternative. This Part will lay out the communitarian and democratic insights discussed above and show how they combine to provide an answer to the *Yoder* problem. It will then consider objections and conclude that they do not seriously threaten the democratic-communitarian analysis. . . .

The Democratic-Communitarian Answer to the *Yoder* Problem

The democratic-communitarian position on *Yoder* . . . holds that *Yoder* was wrongly decided because it took educational decision making power away from the democratic people and gave it to individual parents and to the courts, which were tasked with weighing the competing interests of the parents and the state. In the democratic-communitarian paradigm, judicial inquiry into educational policy should be limited to two questions: (1) was the policy-making procedure fair and democratic?, and (2) was the policy impermissibly motivated by animus toward a group or groups? As long as question (1) is answered in the affirmative and question (2) is answered in the negative, the judiciary's role is over. As we have seen, counter-majoritarian substantive curricular constraints cannot be democratically justified.

But what the courts should do is only half of the question. What advice does the democratic-communitarian view have to offer the conscientious citizen or politician? As we have seen, with a communitarian view of society comes a fear that too much authority will be exercised by high-level sources of value. The conscientious citizen is thus asked to make an honest judgment about how thick the communal norms are at each level and how much those communal norms need to be inculcated through schooling. The citizen is asked to keep in mind that the thickest sources of value will and should be those at the lowest level. This means that the citizen will want to ponder carefully which social values are important to reproduce nation-wide, state-wide, and school district-wide. The citizen will also want to consider whether some topics should not be addressed in schools or should be addressed but with parents having the option to pull their children out of class while that topic is being addressed.

These decisions will entail a judgment that certain topics are properly dealt with by extracurricular value sources. The fact that *Yoder*'s judicially created exemption from generally applicable education laws was illegitimate does not mean that a similar exemption could not have been granted democratically. What was objectionable in *Yoder* was not the decision that some students need not be educated past eighth grade—the proper amount of schooling is a contestable and contested question, and eighth grade is no more arbitrary a line than any other. What was objectionable in *Yoder* was the fact that this contested question was taken out of the hands of the democratic people and given to individual parents and the courts. A democratic majority may decide not to require education past eighth grade, just as it may decide not to require sex education or to allow parents to remove their children from the sex education class. For that matter, a democratic majority may decide not to require any school at all. We may think that some of these decisions are profoundly unwise, but there is no democratic principle which allows us to enshrine our conception of wisdom in the face of a contrary majority.

Likewise, a majority may decide whether or not to allow private schools or home schools to exist. . . . Of course, the democratic-communitarian standard would counsel a citizen or legislator to ponder long and hard before passing a law prohibiting private schooling. In order to support such a law, the citizen would have to satisfy herself that necessary social values could not be effectively inculcated through regulated private schools. If they could be, then the communitarian principle of keeping high-level value sources as thin as possible will require her to vote against the law. Assuming the people do vote to allow private schooling, the question of how tightly to regulate private schools will also be up for democratic resolution.

In short, the democratic-communitarian answer to the *Yoder* problem is to suggest that the problem with *Yoder* was the identity of the decision-maker. The people may democratically choose to allow the Old Order Amish to remove their children from school after eighth grade, or they may choose to require them to satisfy the same educational requirements as all other students. But there is no constitutional principle that allows a court to remove this question from the democratic arena. The democratic-communitarian analysis does, however, suggest that conscientious citizens and legislators should take seriously a request to be exempt from generally applicable education laws and should grant that request unless it would prevent the transmission of what they consider to be important social values.

Objections and Responses

There are three likely objections to the democratic-communitarian analysis presented above. I shall describe and attempt to respond to each.

Objection 1. Under this proposal, most school districts in the country will throw out their biology textbooks and teach creationism.

This objection seems to rest upon the large number of Americans who say they believe in creationism or "guided" evolution. There are two responses to this objection. The first is empirical: it is not at all clear that the democratic people *want* creationism to be taught instead of evolution. It is a perfectly intelligible position to believe in creationism or guided evolution and yet think that it should not be taught in schools. Indeed, consider the recent controversy over the attempt to introduce a brief statement about intelligent design into the biology curriculum in Dover, Pennsylvania. It should be noted, first, that this statement was in addition to the teaching of evolution, not instead of it (the same was true of Kansas's decision "to include challenges to Darwinian theory in the state [educational] standards"). That is, a divided school board opted for a compromise on a contentious issue. This compromise, however, proved unacceptable to the voters. In school board elections held four days after the end of the trial in a suit contesting the legality of the intelligent design statement, eight candidates who ran on a slate opposing adding intelligent design to the curriculum were elected. Not a single candidate who supported intelligent design in the classroom won. In other words, it is not at all clear that voters would choose to eliminate evolution from the classroom and replace it with creationism.

But the second response must be: so what if they did throw out evolution and teach creationism? I believe that any school board that made this decision would be making a horrible mistake, and I would protest against this mistake with every democratic means at my disposal. But why should my objection be privileged over the equally strong sentiments of the majority of my fellow citizens? We have discovered no principle that allows the entrenching of my minority point of view over that of the majority—appeals to neutrality fail, as do appeals to non-repression and non-discrimination. This is not a question of relativism—still believe that my objections to teaching creationism are *right*—it is simply a matter of democratic humility. It is easy to be a democrat when the rest of the *demos* [population] agrees with one's policy choices, but what allows democracy to function is that citizens commit in advance to recognizing the legitimacy of democratic decisions with which they disagree. My objections to teaching creationism or intelligent design, like my fellow citizens' objections to teaching evolution, belong in the public arena. If a fair democratic decision goes against me, then I will have to teach my children about evolution outside of school.

Objection 2. The democratic-communitarian analysis allows for the totalitarian suppression of dissent.

It is the simple fact that I *can* teach my children about evolution—or creationism, or sex, or the novels of [twentieth-century American writer William] Faulkner—outside of a school that prevents democratically controlled education from becoming democratic totalitarianism. . . . Children *do* still learn things that are not taught in school (indeed, they still learn things that are directly opposed to what they are taught in school). . . . Value sources are myriad, and values not learned from one may well be learned from another. Complete democratic control over *one* value source (the schools) is not totalitarian; complete control of one value source over all others . . . is. Moreover, democratic control of education will likely leave significant power in the hands of parents. . . .

Most states have very few regulations on private schools. The democratic impulse is not a totalitarian impulse; decisions that can be left to lower-level decision-makers while still allowing the values of society at large to be inculcated generally are left to the lower-level decision-makers; and dissent continues to flourish.

Objection 3. Under the democratic-communitarian approach, nothing remains of religious freedom.

On the contrary, I would assert that we have seen at least three important elements which form the core of democratic-communitarian religious freedom. First, we have the judicial component. . . . *Church of the Lukumi Babalu Aye* [see Chapter 2 of this book] stands for the proposition that the state may not target a religious group or groups for disfavored treatment. The Court's blessing of inquiries that go behind the text of the law to find animus in its intent gives this principle real teeth. This is a weighty principle—surely, it is at the very core of what we mean when we speak of religious freedom that the state may not punish me *because* I am Jewish or Muslim or Catholic.

The remaining two elements of democratic-communitarian religious freedom may not be judicially enforceable, but that does not make them any less potent. The second is the fact that, in line with the communitarian intuition discussed above, we do tend to exempt religious groups from generally applicable laws when we think that doing so will not be inimical to our attempt to inculcate social values. This takes many forms, ranging from allowing private education and home schooling to exempting wine used for religious purposes from the National Prohibition Act. These exemptions indicate a democratic determination that religious belief as a source of value is important enough to overcome the goal of the otherwise applicable law. A society's willingness seriously to consider claims for such exemptions is an important element of religious freedom.

Finally, religious freedom is protected by our tradition of dissent. . . . The democratic-communitarian theory suggests that school curricular decisions should be made democratically, but it equally suggests that family decisions should be made by the family, church decisions by the church, etc. These institutions can pass on religious values, and they can serve as focal points for political activism in pursuit of democratically granted exemptions from laws which the religious group finds uncongenial. Taken together, these elements form a robust conception of religious freedom.

As continuing debates over religion and school curricula demonstrate, the *Yoder* problem is still very much with us. This should not be surprising—it is a difficult problem, necessitating an examination of some of the deepest principles underpinning our collective life. Thoughtful scholars have heretofore put forward four broad categories of arguments about the *Yoder* problem. There have been arguments both for and against *Yoder* sounding in liberal neutrality, there have been parentalist arguments for *Yoder*, and there have been republican arguments against *Yoder*. In this Article, I have tried to show that, while each of these arguments raises important questions and concerns, each of them is also deeply flawed. As an alternative, I have put forward a democratic-communitarian answer to the *Yoder* problem. I have attempted to show both that this answer corresponds to our communitarian and democratic intuitions, and also that it is able to address the important concerns raised by the other theories. It is my contention that the democratic-communitarian theory provides the best model for how a pluralist democracy can address the intersection of education and religious belief.

> "Yoder *left an indelible mark on such areas as parents' rights, home schooling, and state regulation of religious schools.*"

The Ruling in Favor of the Amish Has Had a Lasting Impact on Religious and Home Schooling

Shawn Francis Peters

Shawn Francis Peters is the coordinator of the University of Wisconsin–Madison Odyssey Project, a humanities program for adults living in poverty. This viewpoint is an excerpt from his book The Yoder Case: Religious Freedom, Education, and Parental Rights. *In it he discusses the impact that the case, which upheld the right of Amish parents to keep their teenage children out of high school, has had on the issues of parental rights, home schooling, and religious schooling in general. Peters also points out that with regard to other issues involving religious liberty, later U.S. Supreme Court decisions undercut some of the principles that were considered established by the* Yoder *case, leading Congress to pass the Religious Freedom Restoration Act.*

In the 1980s and 1990s, the Amish living in [New Glarus, Wisconsin] continued to seek judicial protections for their religious practices and beliefs. The *Yoder* precedent clearly benefited them when they opposed the application of a state law mandating the display of bright red and orange reflective

Shawn Francis Peters, *The Yoder Case: Religious Freedom, Education, and Parental Rights*. Lawrence, KS: University Press of Kansas, 2003.

triangles on slow-moving vehicles (SMVs). In 1996, the Wisconsin Supreme Court ruled that application of the SMV measure to the Amish—who had argued that placing the SMV emblem on their buggies was too "worldly"—violated their religious liberty. In determining that the state constitution's protections of conscience shielded the Amish, the court relied in part on the interpretive framework established by the U.S. Supreme Court in *Yoder* and its forebear, *Sherbert v. Verner* [1963]. *Yoder* had proved similarly important in earlier SMV emblem cases in Kentucky, Ohio, and Michigan.

Members of other faiths found that *Yoder*'s value as a judicial precedent was limited to a certain extent by the widely noted peculiarities of Warren Burger's opinion for the Court. The chief justice's analysis squared with the arguments made by attorney William Ball on behalf of Miller, Yoder, and Yutzy, but it was so narrowly tailored to the Amish that many courts later struggled to apply its holdings to members of different faiths.

In one instance, a group of fundamentalist Christian parents in Tennessee relied on *Yoder* when they asked to have their children excused from assignments involving a textbook they found objectionable on religious grounds. The Sixth Circuit Court of Appeals denied their claim. It asserted that the Supreme Court's opinion in the Amish case "rested on such a singular set of facts that we do not believe it can be held to announce a general rule" pertaining to the First Amendment protection of religious liberty. A New York case regarding home-schooling regulations yielded a similar result, with a federal district court judge maintaining that "the holding in *Yoder* must be limited to its unique facts and does not control the outcome" of the case at hand. Rulings such as these prompted one observer of *Yoder*'s legacy to assert that the opinion "has had a limited impact" in helping individuals who raised religious liberty claims. The opinion's promise, scholar Jay S. Bybee claimed, "has been long on rhetoric and short on substance."

An Effective Precedent for Religious Schools

In some contexts, however, *Yoder* proved to be an invaluable judicial precedent. The decision was particularly effective for attorney William Ball when he defended educators and parents affiliated with fundamentalist Christian schools. In the 1970s and early 1980s, according to one account, backers of these institutions "fought a holy war against state officials" who were attempting to enforce regulations pertaining to curricula and teacher certification. When they faced prosecution for failing to abide by these regulations, fundamentalist Christians in several states, including Ohio and Kentucky, called on Ball to defend them. In these clashes (which often involved, like *Yoder* prosecutions under state compulsory school attendance laws), a main weapon in Ball's arsenal was the precedent he had helped establish in the New Glarus case. "In making their free exercise claim," commented an observer of Ball's efforts in Kentucky, "the fundamentalist schools rely heavily upon the landmark case of *Wisconsin v. Yoder*."

Ball's defense of pastor Levi W. Whisner typified his reliance on the *Yoder* precedent to free Christian schools from many of the constraints of state oversight. In the fall of 1970, Whisner opened a Christian school in Bradford, Ohio, that did not comply with the minimum state standards for elementary schools. Eventually, Whisner and more than a dozen other parents who had enrolled children at the school were indicted on charges similar to those leveled in the *Yoder* case. Ball defended them by essentially recycling the arguments and strategies he had used to defend the New Glarus Amish. (He even went so far as to reuse one of the expert witnesses from the *Yoder* trial, University of Chicago education professor Donald Erickson.)

At the fundamentalists' trial, Ball devoted part of his opening statement to stressing that the defendants, all of them deeply reverent Christians, were "committed by their consciences to enroll their children in a Christian Bible-oriented school." The First Amendment's protection of the free exercise of religion shielded their right to do so, Ball maintained, provided that the school of their choice operated in compliance with reasonable minimum education standards established by the state. In the case at hand, the state was encroaching on the parents' free exercise rights because it was attempting to enforce a dizzying array of unreasonable regulations on the Tabernacle Christian School. Here, Ball alleged, was another lamentable example of religious liberty being compromised by unwarranted state intrusion. Echoing his stance in *Yoder*, he reminded the court that Whisner and the other Tabernacle Christian School parents were not "attacking the compulsory attendance law on its face. Our complaint goes to the application of that statute. . . . A religious liberty claim has been raised."

The defendants were found guilty at trial. But the Ohio Supreme Court, in an opinion that relied in part on the standards articulated by the U.S. Supreme Court in *Yoder*, reversed the parents' convictions in July 1976. According to scholar James Carper, who has written the authoritative study of the case, backers of Christian schools came to view the *Whisner* ruling as "a keystone in their 'battle' to achieve freedom from state regulations and, indirectly, a measure of separation from the mainstream of society."

An Important Precedent for Home Schooling

Advocates of home schooling have treasured the *Yoder* precedent as well. Launched in part by deeply religious parents who hoped to shield their children from the purported dangers of secularism in the public schools, the home-schooling movement took hold in the United States in the late 1960s and early 1970s. By some estimates, as many as one million children were being taught at home by the mid-1990s. The protections of religious liberty and parental rights afforded by *Yo-*

der helped spark that explosive growth. One scholarly commentator concluded that *Yoder* proved to be a "pivotal case" when home-schoolers were forced to defend their programs in court, allowing them to claim that the First Amendment protected their exercise of religion in their choice of schooling for their children.

Champions of parents' rights have also valued *Yoder*. Along with the Supreme Court's opinions in *Meyer v. Nebraska* [1923] and *Pierce v. Society of Sisters* [1925], the *Yoder* ruling became a lodestar for those who believed that too many "innocent families have become the victims of overintrusive government action," as former Republican congressman Bob Dornan put it. Outraged by condom distribution and sex education in the public schools, Dornan helped spearhead the effort to enact federal parents' rights legislation by cosponsoring the Parental Rights and Responsibilities Act in the House of Representatives in 1995. According to Dornan, that measure (which ultimately failed to pass) was intended to establish "a legal standard to determine when the government may and may not interfere with the family. It would essentially prohibit any level of government from infringing on the right of parents to direct the upbringing of their children." As they urged passage of Dornan's bill and analogous measures, such as state parental rights amendments, a vocal coalition of conservative groups invoked *Yoder*'s protection of parent' rights to direct the upbringing and education of their children.

Yoder's Safeguards Were Later Undercut

Although *Yoder* left an indelible mark on such areas as parents' rights, home schooling, and state regulation of religious schools, the core of its constitutional legacy did not prove to be especially durable. In a series of decisions in the final quarter of the twentieth century, the Supreme Court undercut the safeguards for religious liberty it had erected in *Sherbert v.*

Verner and *Yoder*. . . . The justices chipped away at the interpretive framework they had used to shield the religious liberty of the New Glarus Amish.

United States v. Lee demonstrated the limits of *Yoder*'s usefulness as a shield for the Amish from the perils of modernity. Between 1970 and 1977, an Amishman named Edwin Lee farmed and worked as a carpenter in western Pennsylvania. Lee employed several of his co-religionists in his fields and in his carpentry shop, but he did not pay the Social Security taxes required of employers. Lee had religious grounds for refusing to participate in the Social Security System: the Amish faith stressed self-sufficiency, and its members had long spurned the largesse of the government's old-age pension program. In part because of their faith-based objections, self-employed Amish had been exempted by the federal government from paying Social Security taxes in the mid-1960s, but that privilege had not been extended to Amish who employed others, as Lee did. In 1978, the Internal Revenue Service informed Lee that he owed more than $27,000 in back taxes for the men who had been employed on his farm and in his workshop. The Amishman grudgingly paid a fraction of that total (the $91 he owed for the first quarter of 1973) and then filed a suit in federal court in which he maintained that the imposition of Social Security taxes violated his right to the free exercise of religion. His case found its way onto the U.S. Supreme Court's docket during its October 1981 term.

"To maintain an organized society of faiths requires that some religious practices yield to the common good," Chief Justice Warren Burger wrote for the Court's majority in *Lee*. "Religious beliefs can be accommodated . . . but there is a point at which accommodation would 'radically restrict the operating latitude of the legislature.'" According to the chief justice, whereas the circumstances of *Yoder* had lent themselves to permitting a narrow accommodation for members of one particular religious group, the complexities of the tax system involved in *Lee* made providing faith-based exemptions a hopelessly complicated endeavor. Burger noted that if Lee was exempted from contributing taxes to a government program simply because he had a religious objection to its operation, people who had faith-based reservations regarding war might demand an exemption from paying the portion of their taxes earmarked for defense programs. Opening the floodgates to such privileges might overwhelm the federal tax system, Burger warned. "The tax system could not function," he asserted, "if denominations were allowed to challenge the tax system because tax payments were spent in a manner that violates their religious belief."

In *Lee*, this fear of clogging the tax system with endless religious exemption claims tipped the balance in favor of the federal government. "Because the broad public interest in maintaining a sound tax system is of such high order," Burger wrote in reversing the lower court ruling, "religious belief in conflict with the payment of taxes affords no basis for resisting the tax." Adopting a scolding tone at the end of his opinion, the chief justice claimed that although legislators and judges had long recognized the paramount importance of protecting free exercise rights, "every person cannot be shielded from all the burdens incident to exercising every aspect of the right to practice of religious beliefs."

A Dramatic Change in Religious Liberty Rulings

The trend that began in *Lee* reached its culmination in *Employment Division v. Smith* (1990), when the Supreme Court effectively sounded the death knell for *Yoder*. Prior to *Smith*, the justices had evaluated religious liberty claims by weighing the free exercise rights of individuals against the interests of the state. Within this framework, the application of a neutral law to a religious objector might be held unconstitutional if the state lacked a sufficiently compelling interest in enforcing the statute. (*Yoder* had turned on this very point: the state of Wisconsin had lost in part because it failed to demonstrate its interest in mandating an extra two years of schooling.) In *Smith* the Court essentially scrapped the compelling state interest test. Indeed, in his opinion for the Court, Justice Antonin Scalia went so far as to claim that a society that abided by such a standard would be "courting anarchy." Although the Court did not explicitly overturn *Yoder* (it distinguished the Amish case by noting that it had involved both religious liberty and parental rights), its abandonment of the compelling state interest standard compromised one of the ruling's central constitutional legacies. Now, a statute's surface neutrality toward religion was enough to substantiate its constitutionality.

As *Smith* demonstrated, the overall direction of the Supreme Court's religious liberty jurisprudence changed dramatically in the two decades after *Yoder* was handed down. In the Amish school attendance case and its most significant forebear, *Sherbert v. Verner*, the Court forged stout constitutional protections for religious conduct. It did so by applying the highest level of judicial scrutiny to state actions that appeared to infringe on individuals' religious liberty. *Smith* marked the advent of a decidedly less rigorous level of review. Instead of undertaking a close inspection, the Court would now approach the claims of religious objectors by applying a rational basis or reasonableness test—the most permissive standard available—to the state actions at issue. With the justices looking less stringently at their actions, states would have wider latitude to regulate religious conduct.

Responding to claims that *Smith* gutted constitutional protections for religious liberty, Congress passed the Religious Freedom Restoration Act (RFRA) in 1993. There wasn't much doubt as to the measure's purpose: RFRA clearly was meant to circumvent *Smith* by making the compelling state interest test part of federal law. As one observer put it, "Congress believed that religious practice deserved more protection than *Smith*'s constitutional rule gave it," and it attempted to provide the necessary safeguards by essentially turning back the clock to *Yoder*.

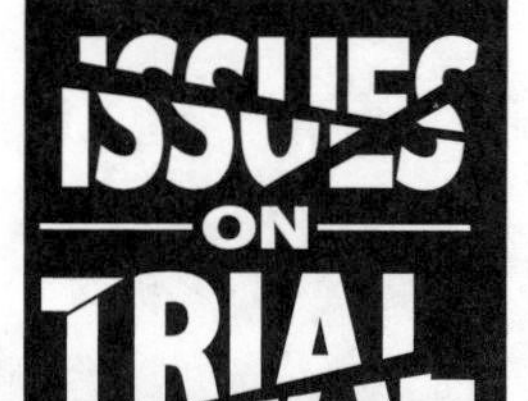

Chapter 2

Balancing Religious Liberty Against Prevailing Public Attitudes

Chapter Preface

Case Overview: *Church of Lukumi Babalu Aye v. City of Hialeah* (1993)

In 1987 Ernesto Pichardo, a priest of the Santeria religion who was in charge of the Church of Lukumi Babalu Aye, announced plans for opening a church in the city of Hialeah, Florida. Previously, members of the church had met only in private homes. Santeria is a minority religion even in Cuba, from which it was brought to the United States by Cuban immigrants. It is based on Lukumi, the African religion of eighteenth-century African slaves in the Caribbean area, combined with Catholicism. Many Cubans, especially the well-educated, look down on it, and it has therefore been practiced somewhat secretively. Pichardo, however, wanted to preserve its traditions and hold public services.

Adherents of Santeria pray both to Catholic saints and to spirits called orishas (Babalu Aye is the name of one of the orishas). They believe that the orishas depend on the sacrifice of animals such as chickens, doves, and goats. In most cases the animals are cooked and eaten after this ritual. Animal sacrifice is not an unusual idea; it is an ancient tradition in many cultures and is mentioned frequently in the Bible.

The citizens of Hialeah strongly opposed the opening of Pichardo's church. Politics, as well as religious objections, were involved. A highly emotional public meeting was held at which outraged speakers condemned animal sacrifice as barbaric. The crowd demanded that something be done to prevent it. The city attorney declared that the rights of all religions are guaranteed by the First Amendment to the U.S. Constitution, but the city council ignored this advice and passed a series of ordinances prohibiting the ritual killing of animals. Pichardo and the church then filed a lawsuit on the grounds that these laws were unconstitutional. The American Civil Liberties Union (ACLU) agreed to pay the expenses of the litigation.

At the district court trial in 1989, the attorney for the city argued that Hialeah's laws applied to all religions, not just Santeria; that they prohibited only conduct, not religious belief; and that there was a compelling governmental interest in protecting public health and preventing cruelty to animals. The trial judge agreed with these arguments and upheld the laws. The case then went to the court of appeals, which issued a brief statement affirming the district court's decision. In 1992 the U.S. Supreme Court granted review of the case. By this time, many large organizations were interested in its implications for religious liberty in general and filed briefs in support of the church, while animal rights organizations filed briefs supporting the city. Much more than the freedom of one small group was at stake.

The main point argued by the attorney for the church—and the basis on which the Supreme Court ultimately overruled the lower courts—was that the city's laws did not affect any animal killing except that connected with religion. Animals could be killed for all sorts of other reasons in Hialeah. "You can kill a turkey in your backyard, put it on the table, say a prayer and serve it for Thanksgiving," said Pichardo. "But if we pray over the turkey, kill it, then eat it, we violated the law."

Contrary to some people's assumption, the 1993 Supreme Court ruling in favor of the church does not mean that animal sacrifice is in itself a constitutionally protected act. A city could prohibit it by passing a law that banned other animal killing as well as the killing of animals for religious purposes. What the Court held was that the Constitution does not allow government to discriminate against religious conduct by imposing bans that are not equally applicable to equivalent conduct performed for nonreligious reasons. It is extremely rare for that to be attempted. The *Lukumi v. Hialeah* case, unlike most religious liberty cases, did not involve exemption from a general law on religious grounds—it was a matter of striking down laws that had no effect other than to suppress the practice of a religion.

"Legislators may not devise mechanisms, overt or disguised, designed to persecute or oppress a religion or its practices."

The Court's Decision: Hialeah's Law Against Animal Sacrifice Was Intended to Suppress a Religion, Not to Protect Animals

Anthony Kennedy

Anthony Kennedy is a justice of the U.S. Supreme Court. The following viewpoint is the Court's majority opinion in the case of Church of Lukumi Babalu Aye v. City of Hialeah. *(Although all the justices agreed with the ruling, some of them disagreed with the details of the arguments for it and filed separate opinions.) The Court determined that although the laws of the city of Hialeah, Florida, against animal sacrifice were ostensibly passed to protect public health and prevent cruelty to animals, they were actually designed to suppress the Santeria religion. Many other forms of animal killing in Hialeah were not affected by these laws, yet for a law that interferes with a religious practice to be legal under the Constitution, it must also apply in situations not connected to religion. Therefore, the Court ruled that the laws in question were void.*

The principle that government may not enact laws that suppress religious belief or practice is so well understood that few violations are recorded in our opinions. Concerned

Anthony Kennedy, majority opinion, *Church of Lukumi Babalu Aye v. City of Hialeah*, U.S. Supreme Court, June 11, 1993.

that this fundamental nonpersecution principle of the First Amendment was implicated here, however, we granted certiorari [review].

Our review confirms that the laws in question were enacted by officials who did not understand, failed to perceive, or chose to ignore the fact that their official actions violated the Nation's essential commitment to religious freedom. The challenged laws had an impermissible object; and in all events, the principle of general applicability was violated because the secular ends asserted in defense of the laws were pursued only with respect to conduct motivated by religious beliefs. We invalidate the challenged enactments, and reverse the judgment of the Court of Appeals.

This case involves practices of the Santeria religion, which originated in the 19th century. When hundreds of thousands of members of the Yoruba people were brought as slaves from western Africa to Cuba, their traditional African religion absorbed significant elements of Roman Catholicism. The resulting syncretion, or fusion, is Santeria, "the way of the saints." The Cuban Yoruba express their devotion to spirits, called orishas, through the iconography of Catholic saints, Catholic symbols are often present at Santeria rites, and Santeria devotees attend the Catholic sacraments. . . .

The Santeria faith teaches that every individual has a destiny from God, a destiny fulfilled with the aid and energy of the orishas. The basis of the Santeria religion is the nurture of a personal relation with the orishas, and one of the principal forms of devotion is an animal sacrifice. The sacrifice of animals as part of religious rituals has ancient roots. . . .

According to Santeria teaching, the orishas are powerful, but not immortal. They depend for survival on the sacrifice. Sacrifices are performed at birth, marriage, and death rites, for the cure of the sick, for the initiation of new members and priests, and during an annual celebration. Animals sacrificed in Santeria rituals include chickens, pigeons, doves, ducks, guinea pigs, goats, sheep, and turtles. The animals are killed by the cutting of the carotid arteries in the neck. The sacrificed animal is cooked and eaten, except after healing and death rituals.

Santeria adherents faced widespread persecution in Cuba, so the religion and its rituals were practiced in secret. The open practice of Santeria and its rites remains infrequent. The religion was brought to this Nation most often by exiles from the Cuban revolution. The District Court estimated that there are at least 50,000 practitioners in South Florida today.

Petitioner Church of the Lukumi Babalu Aye, Inc. (Church), is a not-for-profit corporation organized under Florida law in 1973. The Church and its congregants practice the Santeria religion. . . .

In April, 1987, the Church leased land in the city of Hialeah, Florida, and announced plans to establish a house of worship as well as a school, cultural center, and museum. . . .

The City Council's Action

The prospect of a Santeria church in their midst was distressing to many members of the Hialeah community, and the announcement of the plans to open a Santeria church in Hialeah prompted the city council to hold an emergency public session on June 9, 1987. . . .

First, the city council adopted Resolution 87-66, which noted the "concern" expressed by residents of the city "that certain religions may propose to engage in practices which are inconsistent with public morals, peace or safety," and declared that "the City reiterates its commitment to a prohibition against any and all acts of any and all religious groups which are inconsistent with public morals, peace or safety." Next, the council approved an emergency ordinance, Ordinance 87-40, which incorporated in full, except as to penalty, Florida's animal cruelty laws. . . .

Florida law prohibited a municipality from enacting legislation relating to animal cruelty that conflicted with state law. To obtain clarification, Hialeah's city attorney requested an opinion from the attorney general of Florida as to whether [state law] prohibited "a religious group from sacrificing an animal in a religious ritual or practice," and whether the city could enact ordinances "making religious animal sacrifice unlawful." The attorney general . . . concluded that the "ritual sacrifice of animals for purposes other than food consumption" was not a "necessary" killing, and so was prohibited. The attorney general appeared to define "unnecessary" as "done without any useful motive, in a spirit of wanton cruelty or for the mere pleasure of destruction without being in any sense beneficial or useful to the person killing the animal." . . .

In September, 1987, the city council adopted three substantive ordinances addressing the issue of religious animal sacrifice. Ordinance 87-52 defined "sacrifice" as "to unnecessarily kill, torment, torture, or mutilate an animal in a public or private ritual or ceremony not for the primary purpose of food consumption," and prohibited owning or possessing an animal "intending to use such animal for food purposes." It restricted application of this prohibition, however, to any individual or group that "kills, slaughters or sacrifices animals for any type of ritual, regardless of whether or not the flesh or blood of the animal is to be consumed." The ordinance contained an exemption for slaughtering by "licensed establishment[s]" of animals "specifically raised for food purposes." Declaring, moreover, that the city council has determined that the sacrificing of animals within the city limits is contrary to the public health, safety, welfare and morals of the community, the city council adopted Ordinance 87-71. . . .

The District Court's Decision

Following enactment of these ordinances, the Church and [its priest Ernesto] Pichardo filed his action pursuant to 42 U.S.C. 1983 in the United States District Court for the Southern District of Florida. . . .

The court found four compelling [governmental] interests. First, the court found that animal sacrifices present a substantial health risk, both to participants and the general public. According to the court, animals that are to be sacrificed are often kept in unsanitary conditions and are uninspected, and animal remains are found in public places. Second, the court found emotional injury to children who witness the sacrifice of animals. Third, the court found compelling the city's interest in protecting animals from cruel and unnecessary killing. The court determined that the method of killing used in Santeria sacrifice was "unreliable and not humane, and that the animals, before being sacrificed, are often kept in conditions that produce a great deal of fear and stress in the animal." Fourth, the District Court found compelling the city's interest in restricting the slaughter or sacrifice of animals to areas zoned for slaughterhouse use. . . .

Balancing the competing governmental and religious interests, the District Court concluded the compelling governmental interests "fully justify the absolute prohibition on ritual sacrifice" accomplished by the ordinances. Id., at 1487. The court also concluded that an exception to the sacrifice prohibition for religious conduct would "'unduly interfere with fulfillment of the governmental interest'" because any more narrow restrictions—e.g., regulation of disposal of animal carcasses—would be unenforceable as a result of the secret nature of the Santeria religion. . . .

The Court of Appeals for the Eleventh Circuit affirmed [this decision]. . . . Choosing not to rely on the District Court's recitation of a compelling interest in promoting the welfare of children, the Court of Appeals stated simply that it concluded the ordinances were consistent with the Constitution. . . .

The city does not argue that Santeria is not a "religion" within the meaning of the First Amendment. Nor could it. Although the practice of animal sacrifice may seem abhorrent to some, "religious beliefs need not be acceptable, logical, consistent, or comprehensible to others in order to merit First Amendment protection." *Thomas v. Review Bd. of Indiana Employment Security Div., 450 U.S. 707, 714* (1981). Given the historical association between animal sacrifice and religious worship, petitioners' assertion that animal sacrifice is an integral part of their religion "cannot be deemed bizarre or incredible." *Frezee v. Illinois Dept. of Employment Security, 480 U.S. 829, 834*, n. 2 (1989). Neither the city nor the courts below, moreover, have questioned the sincerity of petitioners' professed desire to conduct animal sacrifices for religious reasons. We must consider petitioners' First Amendment claim.

In addressing the constitutional protection for free exercise of religion, our cases establish the general proposition that [a law that is neutral and of general applicability need not be justified by a compelling governmental interest even if the law has the incidental effect of burdening a particular religious practice]. Neutrality and general applicability are interrelated, and, as becomes apparent in this case, failure to satisfy one requirement is a likely indication that the other has not been satisfied. A law failing to satisfy these requirements must be justified by a compelling governmental interest, and must be narrowly tailored to advance that interest. These ordinances [fail to satisfy the Smith requirements.]...

In our Establishment Clause cases, we have often stated the principle that the First Amendment forbids an official purpose to disapprove of a particular religion or of religion in general....

At a minimum, the protections of the Free Exercise Clause pertain if the law at issue discriminates against some or all religious beliefs or regulates or prohibits conduct because it is undertaken for religious reason....

Suppression of Santeria Was the Object of the City Laws

The record in this case compels the conclusion that suppression of the central element of the Santeria worship service was the object of the ordinances. First, though use of the words "sacrifice" and "ritual" does not compel a finding of improper targeting of the Santeria religion, the choice of these words is support for our conclusion. There are further respects in which the text of the city council's enactments discloses the improper attempt to target Santeria. Resolution 87-66, adopted June 9, 1987, recited that "residents and citizens of the City of Hialeah have expressed their concern that certain religions may propose to engage in practices which are inconsistent with public morals, peace or safety," and "reiterate[d]" the city's commitment to prohibit "any and all [such] acts of any and all religious groups." No one suggests, and, on this record, it cannot be maintained, that city officials had in mind a religion other than Santeria.

It becomes evident that these ordinances target Santeria sacrifice when the ordinances' operation is considered. Apart from the text, the effect of a law in its real operation is strong evidence of its object. . . .

It is a necessary conclusion that almost the only conduct subject to Ordinances 87-40, 87-52, and 87-71 is the religious exercise of Santeria church members. The texts show that they were drafted in tandem to achieve this result. . . .

Indeed, careful drafting ensured that, although Santeria sacrifice is prohibited, killings that are no more necessary or humane in almost all other circumstances are unpunished.

Operating in similar fashion is Ordinance 87-52, which prohibits the "possess[ion], sacrifice, or slaughter" of an animal with the "inten[t] to use such animal for food purposes." This prohibition, extending to the keeping of an animal, as well as the killing itself, applies if the animal is killed in "any type of ritual" and there is an intent to use the animal for food, whether or not it is in fact consumed for food. The ordinance exempts, however, "any licensed [food] establishment" with regard to "any animals which are specifically raised for food purposes," if the activity is permitted by zoning and other laws. This exception, too, seems intended to cover Kosher [ritual Jewish] slaughter. Again, the burden of the ordinance, in practical terms, falls on Santeria adherents, but almost no others. . . .

Ordinance 87-40 incorporates the Florida animal cruelty statute. Its prohibition is broad on its face, punishing "whoever . . . unnecessarily . . . kills any animal." The city claims that this ordinance is the epitome of a neutral prohibition. The problem, however, is the interpretation given to the ordinance by respondent and the Florida attorney general. Killings for religious reasons are deemed unnecessary, whereas most other killings fall outside the prohibition. The city, on what seems to be a per se basis, deems hunting, slaughter of animals for food, eradication of insects and pests, and euthanasia as necessary. There is no indication in the record that respondent has concluded that hunting or fishing for sport is unnecessary. Indeed, one of the few reported Florida cases decided under [state law] concludes that the use of live rabbits to train greyhounds is not unnecessary. . . .

We also find significant evidence of the ordinances' improper targeting of Santeria sacrifice in the fact that they proscribe more religious conduct than is necessary to achieve their stated ends. It is not unreasonable to infer, at least when there are no persuasive indications to the contrary, that a law which visits "gratuitous restrictions" on religious conduct seeks not to effectuate the stated governmental interests, but to suppress the conduct because of its religious motivation.

The [legitimate governmental interests in protecting the public health and preventing cruelty to animals could be addressed by restrictions stopping far short of a flat prohibition of all Santeria sacrificial practice.] If improper disposal, not the sacrifice itself, is the harm to be prevented, the city could have imposed a general regulation on the disposal of organic garbage. . . . The District Court accepted the argument that narrower regulation would be unenforceable because of the secrecy in the Santeria rituals and the lack of any central religious authority to require compliance with secular disposal regulations. It is difficult to understand, however, how a prohibition of the sacrifices themselves, which occur in private, is enforceable if a ban on improper disposal, which occurs in public, is not. The neutrality of a law is suspect if First Amendment freedoms are curtailed to prevent isolated collateral harms not themselves prohibited by direct regulation.

Under similar analysis, narrower regulation would achieve the city's interest in preventing cruelty to animals. With regard to the city's interest in ensuring the adequate care of animals, regulation of conditions and treatment, regardless of why an animal is kept, is the logical response to the city's concern, not a prohibition on possession for the purpose of sacrifice. The same is true for the city's interest in prohibiting cruel methods of killing. Under federal and Florida law and Ordinance 87-40, which incorporates Florida law in this regard, killing an animal by the "simultaneous and instantaneous severance of the carotid arteries with a sharp instrument"—the method used in kosher slaughter—is approved as humane. The District Court found that, though Santeria sacrifice also results in severance of the carotid arteries, the method used during sacrifice is less reliable, and therefore not humane. If the city has a real concern that other methods are less humane, however, the subject of the regulation should be the method of slaughter itself, not a religious classification that is said to bear some general relation to it. . . .

That the ordinances were enacted "'because of,' not merely 'in spite of,'" their suppression of Santeria religious practice, is revealed by the events preceding enactment. . . . The minutes and taped excerpts of the June 9 session, both of which are in the record, evidence significant hostility exhibited by residents, members of the city council, and other city officials toward the Santeria religion and its practice of animal sacrifice. . . .

Councilman [Silvio] Cardoso said that Santeria devotees at the Church "are in violation of everything this country stands for." Councilman [Andres] Mejides indicated that he was "totally against the sacrificing of animals," and distinguished kosher slaughter because it had a "real purpose.". . . Councilman [Herman] Echevarria asked: "What can we do to prevent the Church from opening?"

Various Hialeah city officials made comparable comments. The chaplain of the Hialeah Police Department told the city council that Santeria was a sin, "foolishness," "an abomination to the Lord," and the worship of "demons.". . . He concluded: "I would exhort you . . . not to permit this Church to exist." The city attorney commented that Resolution 87-66 indicated: "This community will not tolerate religious practices which are abhorrent to its citizens." . . .

In sum, the neutrality inquiry leads to one conclusion: the ordinances had as their object the suppression of religion. The pattern we have recited discloses animosity to Santeria adherents and their religious practices; the ordinances, by their own terms, target this religious exercise; the texts of the ordinances were gerrymandered with care to proscribe religious killings of animals but to exclude almost all secular killings; and the ordinances suppress much more religious conduct than is necessary in order to achieve the legitimate ends asserted in their defense. These ordinances are not neutral, and the court below committed clear error in failing to reach this conclusion.

Other Ways of Killing Animals Are Not Prohibited

We turn next to a second requirement of the Free Exercise Clause, the rule that laws burdening religious practice must be of general applicability. . . . The principle that government, in pursuit of legitimate interests, cannot in a selective manner impose burdens only on conduct motivated by religious belief essential to the protection of the rights guaranteed by the Free Exercise Clause. . . .

Respondent claims that Ordinances 87-40, 87-52, and 87-71 advance two interests: protecting the public health and preventing cruelty to animals. The ordinances are underinclusive for those ends. They fail to prohibit nonreligious conduct that endangers these interests in a similar or greater degree than Santeria sacrifice does. The underinclusion is substantial, not inconsequential. Despite the city's proffered interest in preventing cruelty to animals, the ordinances are drafted with care to forbid few killings but those occasioned by religious sacrifice. Many types of animal deaths or kills for nonreligious reasons are either not prohibited or approved by express provision. For example, fishing—which occurs in Hialeah—is legal. Extermination of mice and rats within a home is also permitted. Florida law sanctions euthanasia of "stray, neglected, abandoned, or unwanted animals," destruction of animals judicially removed from their owners "for humanitarian reasons" or when the animal "is of no commercial value," the infliction of pain or suffering "in the interest of medical science," the placing of poison in one's yard or enclosure, and the use of live animals "to pursue or take wildlife or to participate in any hunting," and "to hunt wild hogs". . . .

The ordinances are also underinclusive with regard to the city's interest in public health, which is threatened by the disposal of animal carcasses in open public places and the consumption of uninspected meat. Neither interest is pursued by respondent with regard to conduct that is not motivated by religious conviction. The health risks posed by the improper disposal of animal carcasses are the same whether Santeria sacrifice or some nonreligious killing preceded it. The city does not, however, prohibit hunters from bringing their kill to their houses, nor does it regulate disposal after their activity. Despite substantial testimony at trial that the same public health hazards result from improper disposal of garbage by restaurants, restaurants are outside the scope of the ordinances. . . .

The ordinances are underinclusive as well with regard to the health risk posed by consumption of uninspected meat. Under the city's ordinances, hunters may eat their kill and fishermen may eat their catch without undergoing governmental inspection. Likewise, state law requires inspection of meat that is sold, but exempts meat from animals raised for the use of the owner and "members of his household and nonpaying guests and employees." The asserted interest in inspected meat is not pursued in contexts similar to that of religious animal sacrifice.

Ordinance 87-72, which prohibits the slaughter of animals outside of areas zoned for slaughterness, is underinclusive on its face. . . . Respondent has not explained why commercial operations that slaughter "small numbers" of hogs and cattle do not implicate its professed desire to prevent cruelty to animals and preserve the public health. Although the city has classified Santeria sacrifice as slaughter, subjecting it to this ordinance, it does not regulate other killings for food in like manner.

Law Must Not Target Religious Conduct

We conclude, in sum, that each of Hialeah's ordinances pursues the city's governmental interests only against conduct motivated by religious belief. The ordinances "ha[ve] every appearance of a prohibition that society is prepared to impose upon [Santeria worshippers] but not upon itself." This precise evil is what the requirement of general applicability is designed to prevent.

A law burdening religious practice that is not neutral or not of general application must undergo the most rigorous of scrutiny. To satisfy the commands of the First Amendment, a law restrictive of religious practice must advance "'interest of the highest order,'" and must be narrowly tailored in pursuit of those interest. *McDaniel v. Paty*. . . . A law that targets religious conduct for distinctive treatment or advances legitimate governmental interests only against conduct with a religious motivation will survive strict scrutiny only in rare cases. It follows from what we have already said that these ordinances cannot withstand this scrutiny. . . .

The Free Exercise Clause commits government itself to religious tolerance, and upon even slight suspicion that proposals for state intervention stem from animosity to religion or distrust of its practices, all officials must pause to remember their own high duty to the Constitution and to the rights it secures. Those in office must be resolute in resisting importunate demands and must ensure that the sole reasons for imposing the burdens of law and regulation are secular. Legislator may not devise mechanisms, overt or disguised, designed to persecute or oppress a religion or its practices. The laws here in question were enacted contrary to these constitutional principles, and they are void.

"This case does not present . . . the question whether the Free Exercise Clause would require a religious exemption from a law that sincerely pursued the goal of protecting animals from cruel treatment."

Concurring Opinion: The Court Made the Right Judgment for the Wrong Reason

Harry Blackmun

Harry Blackmun was a justice of the U.S. Supreme Court. The following viewpoint is his opinion in the Hialeah *case, which was joined by Justice Sandra Day O'Connor, in which he concurs with the Court's judgment but disagrees with the basis on which it was made. The precedent cited in this case,* Employment Division v. Smith, *was one with which many people, including Justice Blackmun, (who had dissented from the decision in that case) disagreed because, as he says here, "it ignored the value of religious freedom as an affirmative individual liberty, and treated the Free Exercise Clause as no more than an anti-discrimination principle." In addition, he points out that the* Hialeah *case would have been harder to decide if it had involved a claim of religious exemption from a general law designed to prevent cruelty to animals, instead of one that specifically targeted the practice of a religion.*

Harry Blackmun, concurring opinion, *Church of Lukumi Babalu Aye v. City of Hialeah*, U.S. Supreme Court, June 11, 1993.

The Court holds today that the city of Hialeah violated the First and Fourteenth Amendments when it passed a set of restrictive ordinances explicitly directed at petitioners' religious practice. With this holding, I agree. I write separately to emphasize that the First Amendment's protection of religion extends beyond those rare occasions on which the government explicitly targets religion (or a particular religion) for disfavored treatment, as is done in this case. In my view, a statute that burdens the free exercise of religion "may stand only if the law in general, and the State's refusal to allow a religious exemption in particular, are justified by a compelling interest that cannot be served by less restrictive means." *Employment Div., Dept. of Human Resources of Ore. v. Smith* (1990) (dissenting opinion). The Court, however, applies a different test. It applies the test announced in Smith, under which "a law that is neutral and of general applicability need not be justified by a compelling governmental interest even if the law has the incidental effect of burdening a particular religious practice." I continue to believe that *Smith* was wrongly decided, because it ignored the value of religious freedom as an affirmative individual liberty, and treated the Free Exercise Clause as no more than an antidiscrimination principle. Thus, while I agree with the result the Court reaches in this case, I arrive at that result by a different route.

When the State enacts legislation that intentionally or unintentionally places a burden upon religiously motivated practice, it must justify that burden by "showing that it is the least restrictive means of achieving some compelling state interest." *Thomas v. Review Bd. of Indiana Employment Security Div.* (1981). See also *Wisconsin v. Yoder*. A State may no more create an underinclusive statute, one that fails truly to promote its purported compelling interest, than it may create an overinclusive statute, one that encompasses more protected conduct than necessary to achieve its goal. In the latter circumstance, the broad scope of the statute is unnecessary to serve the interest, and the statute fails for that reason. In the former situation, the fact that allegedly harmful conduct falls outside the statute's scope belies a governmental assertion that it has genuinely pursued an interest "of the highest order." If the State's goal is important enough to prohibit religiously motivated activity, it will not and must not stop at religiously motivated activity. . . .

In this case, the ordinances at issue are both overinclusive and underinclusive in relation to the state interests they purportedly serve. They are overinclusive, as the majority correctly explains, because the "legitimate governmental interests in protecting the public health and preventing cruelty to animals could be addressed by restrictions stopping far short of a flat prohibition of all Santeria sacrificial practice." They are underinclusive as well, because, "despite the city's proffered interest in preventing cruelty to animals, the ordinances are drafted with care to forbid few killings but those occasioned by religious sacrifice." Moreover, the "ordinances are also underinclusive with regard to the city's interest in public health. . . ."

When a law discriminates against religion as such, as do the ordinances in this case, it automatically will fail strict scrutiny under *Sherbert v. Verner* (holding that governmental regulation that imposes a burden upon religious practice must be narrowly tailored to advance a compelling state interest). This is true because a law that targets religious practice for disfavored treatment both burdens the free exercise of religion and, by definition, is not precisely tailored to a compelling governmental interest.

The Case Is Easy to Decide

Thus, unlike the majority, I do not believe that "a law burdening religious practice that is not neutral or not of general application must undergo the most rigorous of scrutiny." In my view, regulation that targets religion in this way, ipso facto [by that very fact], fails strict scrutiny. It is for this reason that a statute that explicitly restricts religious practices violates the First Amendment. Otherwise, however, "the First Amendment . . . does not distinguish between laws that are generally applicable and laws that target particular religious practices." *Smith* (opinion concurring in judgment).

It is only in the rare case that a state or local legislature will enact a law directly burdening religious practice as such. Because respondent here does single out religion in this way, the present case is an easy one to decide.

A harder case would be presented if petitioners were requesting an exemption from a generally applicable anticruelty law. The result in the case before the Court today, and the fact that every Member of the Court concurs in that result, does not necessarily reflect this Court's views of the strength of a State's interest in prohibiting cruelty to animals. This case does not present, and I therefore decline to reach, the question whether the Free Exercise Clause would require a religious exemption from a law that sincerely pursued the goal of protecting animals from cruel treatment. The number of organizations that have filed amicus [friend of the court] briefs on behalf of this interest, however, demonstrates that it is not a concern to be treated lightly.

"The Free Exercise Clause . . . guarantees that believers of every faith, and not just the majority, are able to practice their religion without unnecessary interference from the government."

Minority Religions Are the Ones Most in Need of Constitutional Protection

Robert F. Drinan and Jennifer I. Huffman

Robert F. Drinan is a professor of law at Georgetown University Law Center. He is a former member of the U.S. House of Representatives and has published several books. Jennifer I. Huffman was a law student at the time this article was written and is now an attorney. In the following viewpoint, written after the U.S. Supreme Court had heard the Hialeah *case but before its decision had been made, they explain why animal sacrifice is important in the Santeria religion and why they believe the lower courts were wrong to uphold the City of Hialeah's attempt to ban it. They also discuss the precedent established by an earlier case,* Employment Division of Oregon v. Smith, *which was widely criticized for restricting religious liberty, and express their hope that the Court would not interpret* Smith *as requiring a ruling against a small, unpopular religion of the kind most in need of constitutional protection.*

In a Christian church, the sacrament of communion is an integral rite of the faith. Similarly, in Judaism, eating kosher food is for many followers a required part of their faith. And in Santeria, a four thousand-year-old African religion now practiced in the United States, an essential aspect of worship is animal sacrifice. Though the practice of animal sacrifice to many people in the United States may seem strange or primitive, to the followers of Santeria it is a necessary part of their relationship with their gods.

In response to the opening of a Santeria church, a city in Florida placed an outright ban on the ritual sacrifice of animals. The Santeria church and its priest took the city to court, claiming a violation of their First Amendment free exercise rights. The case made its way to the U.S. Supreme Court and on 4 November 1992 the Court heard oral arguments. The parties now await the Court's decision on whether the First Amendment protects the Santeria followers' right to worship. . . .

The issues at stake in Church of the Lukumi go beyond the sensationalism of animal sacrifice and a mysterious ancient religion to all religions' freedom to worship. However, perhaps more importantly, it is such a small, exotic religion as Santeria that the Free Exercise Clause and the Supreme Court must protect.

The Santeria Religion

The members of the church of the Lukumi Babalu Aye are followers of Santeria, or Yoruba as it is also known, a four thousand-year-old religion that originated in West Africa and was first brought to the Caribbean with slavery approximately four hundred years ago. The religion came to the United States in the 1950s and 1960s with Cubans who fled Fidel Castro's communist government. Practitioners of Santeria in the United States are located primarily in South Florida, New York City, and Los Angeles. The religion has continued to grow among the Cuban population in the United States, often because it has been a source of support and comfort for refugees facing a new and difficult life in a new country.

The basis of Santeria is the individual's relationship with the orishas or spirits. An integral part of the development of this relationship, and of paying homage to the orishas, is the practice of animal sacrifice. Chickens, pigeons, doves, ducks, guinea fowl, goats, sheep, and turtles are sacrificed in ceremonies for the initiation of new priests, for birth, marriage, and death, for healing purposes, and for certain annual celebrations. Most of the animals, except those used in the rites for death or sickness, are cooked and eaten. The actual sacrifice is performed by a priest who uses a knife to sever the arteries in the neck of the animal. "The slaughter is always performed quickly and cleanly according to ritual rules." . . .

Many Cuban-Americans are embarrassed by Santeria, a "primitive" religion, and believe that it reflects badly on them. Santeria has thus remained an underground religion practiced in private homes and its practitioners often do not know the identity of other practitioners. . . .

It was the secretive nature of the practice of Santeria and the continuing discrimination which Ernesto Pichardo hoped to challenge by opening a permanent, public Santeria Church in Hialeah. Pichardo, a priest of the Church of Lukumi Babalu Aye, asserted that "as long as we continue to practice in our homes, we will continue to reinforce the idea that this [religion] is not worthwhile and that it is a secretive form of worship." Early in 1987 Pichardo's church announced plans to open in a used car lot in Hialeah what would be the first ever North American Santeria church. This announcement was greeted with a storm of protest from Hialeah residents. Some of the concerns regarding the disposal of animal carcasses were legitimate: Pichardo addressed these concerns with plans for an incinerator on the property. Indeed, having the worship and sacrifice occur in one location instead of in many anonymous private homes should make the disposal problem much easier to control.

However, many of the sentiments expressed in opposition to the church's opening were not legitimate and revealed the ignorance and discrimination that have long surrounded Santeria. Neighbors worried that pets would be sacrificed; however, practitioners of Santeria purchase their animals and do not sacrifice dogs and cats. The church was widely accused of worshipping the devil. A local Baptist minister called animal sacrifice "indefensible and repugnant" in "our civilized society." The director of the regional humane society office referred to Santeria as "a bloody cult . . . whose continued presence further blights the image of South Florida."

Thus the public response to the new church, the vehemence of which would prompt city officials to pass the ordinances, was not primarily motivated by the "compelling state interests" later given by the city in court. Instead the outcry was fueled by misconceptions about Santeria and discrimination against the exotic, minority religion. . . .

The Effect of the *Smith* Decision

The Supreme Court's decision to hear *Church of the Lukumi* created a great deal of speculation and attention because, with this case, the Court will most likely attempt to define and clarify the *Smith* decision and current free exercise law. *Church of the Lukumi* is the first free exercise case the Court has agreed to hear since [*Employment Division of Oregon v.*] *Smith*. In *Smith*, two members of the Native American Church were fired from their private drug counseling jobs for ingesting peyote as part of a religious ceremony. The State of Oregon then denied the church members' unemployment compensation claims because the members were fired for work-related "misconduct." The members' claim that this denial violated their First Amendment free exercise rights was ultimately denied by the Supreme Court.

Justice Antonin Scalia, writing for the majority, found that the Oregon laws prohibiting the possession and/or use of controlled substances including peyote did not specifically target religion, but were neutral and generally applicable. The prevailing method of analyzing free exercise claims prior to this case had been to balance the *state* interests advanced by the government action against the individual's right to free exercise of religion. However, the majority opinion of *Smith* interpreted the precedents to mean that the compelling interest test has only been applicable in the context of unemployment compensation claims. In other contexts, the sole question is whether the law in question is neutral and generally applicable. Across-the-board criminal prohibitions are within the police powers of a *state*. Therefore, in *Smith*, no weighing of the *state's* compelling interests had to be performed, and because the drug laws were applicable to everyone, they were held not to be unconstitutional.

Legal scholars have been largely consistent in condemning the *Smith* result. *Smith* has been decried for a number of reasons, from the distortion of precedents and history to the concern that *Smith* puts all religious practices at the mercy of the majority. What has perhaps been more surprising than the opposition of scholars to *Smith* has been the vehement opposition of large numbers of religious groups. Many diverse religions, often on opposing sides on other issues, have rallied together to fight what they see as a fundamental assault on their constitutional right to freedom of religion. There have been alliances in the courtroom: the Hare Krishnas, for example, in their partially successful effort to have the right to solicit funds and hand out literature at New York airports were supported by the American Jewish Congress, the Catholic League for Religious and Civil Rights, and the National Council of Evangelicals, among others.

In addition, religious groups have come together to support the Religious Freedom Restoration Act. This bill, the subject of the House Subcommittee on Civil and Constitutional Rights hearings and approved for full Judiciary Committee action on 24 June 1992, would simply return free exercise law to where it was before *Smith*. That is, a law which restricts the free exercise of religion must show both a compelling state interest and that the law is the least restrictive means to further that interest.

A survey of post-*Smith* free exercise cases in the lower federal and state courts tells an ominous tale of religious practices losing protection they might have had before *Smith*. Even while following the precedent set by *Smith*, federal judges have expressed disapproval and dismay over the opinion.

The District Court's Opinion

At a time, then, when a great deal of attention was focused on the Supreme Court's free exercise policy, the Court granted certiorari [agreed to review] in March 1991 to an unlikely case out of Southern Florida. From the beginning of the Church of the Lukumi Babalu Aye's clashes with the City of Hialeah, the participants recognized that this was more than a simple fight over a municipal ordinance. The issue was religious freedom and a question never before addressed by the courts: Is the practice of animal sacrifice protected under the Free Exercise Clause of the First Amendment.

The nine-day trial in which the district court tried to answer this question was marked by the same accusations and emotions that occurred at the city council meetings. . . .

The district court's opinion is troubling for several reasons. It gives a disapproving description of the church and its nonconventional background, seemingly because Santeria worship is secretive, and the church has no written official doctrine, no centralized authority, and thus no certification procedures for its priests. . . .

The opinion is also troubling because it emphasizes more than once that the Hialeah animal sacrifice ordinances regulate conduct, not belief, and thus the implication is that a religious practice is not protected by the First Amendment. The

Supreme Court, however, in 1940 established that laws regulating religious conduct can violate the Free Exercise Clause of the First Amendment. *Smith*, despite narrowing the scope of free exercise review in general, reconfirms this holding. . . .

The district court found that the Hialeah ordinances were not religiously neutral, because the city intended to stop the Santeria religious practice. The city's intent is further evidenced by the circumstances surrounding the passage of the ordinances. The concerns given in court by Hialeah—health hazards, psychological effects on children, and cruelty to animals—were present when Santeria was only being practiced in private homes. However, the city only addressed these concerns after the church had announced plans to open a public church which the community violently opposed. . . .

When weighing governmental versus religious interest, one principle that has been returned to consistently in free exercise cases is the idea of the "least restrictive means." The government's interest which is advanced by the law in question must not only be compelling, but the law must be the least restrictive means to meet this interest. . . .

In the case of the City of Hialeah and the Santeria religion, the interests put forth by the city as being advanced by the ordinances can (and should) be addressed by measures less drastic than a complete ban on the Santeria followers' religious practice. The city's three primary purposes in enacting the ordinances, as found by the district court, were "the perceived need to prevent cruelty to animals, to safeguard the health, welfare and safety of the community, and to prevent possible adverse psychological effects on children exposed to such sacrifices." The court of appeals did not accept this third interest so it is necessary to consider only the first two.

In discussing the city's interest in banning animal sacrifice to prevent a health hazard, the district court found that "It is beyond dispute that the government has a compelling interest in controlling disease." While this is certainly true, and dead animals can harbor disease-causing germs, there is little evidence that banning animal sacrifice will have any marked effect on the public health. The district court found "There have been no instances documented of any infectious disease originating from the remains of animals being left in public places." Testimony at the trial revealed that the public health threat from dead animals comes from many sources: animal parts in restaurant garbages, dead rats, and animals killed on the roads. "Thus, according to the record evidence, the problem of improperly discarded sacrificial animals is a small part of the problem of dead animals, which in turn is a very small part of the problem of organic garbage." This being the case, banning all animal sacrifice to address this public health hazard is both gross overkill and ineffective. Laws simply prescribing the proper, required method of disposal of carcasses would be sufficient. Therefore, the city not only failed to use the least restrictive means to address this interest, it also failed to show a compelling state interest of a public health hazard which must be addressed by a ban on sacrifice.

Hialeah Allows Other Forms of Animal Killing

The city's professed interest in the prevention of cruelty to animals is curious. The least restrictive means standard is not helpful here, because if the city's interest in preventing the killing of animals is compelling, then obviously a ban on sacrifice is necessary to advance this interest. However, the facts show that this professed interest of Hialeah is not compelling. As previously mentioned, the state attorney general found that animal sacrifices are "unnecessary" killings. The district court accepted this judgment of a religious practice without question. However, "the necessity of sacrifice is a theological judgment that no governmental unit can make." Further, the opinion offers no discussion of the many secular forms of animal killing which are legal in Hialeah. Are hunting, trapping, and boiling lobsters alive more "necessary" than a central religious practice of an ancient religion? The fact that so many secular forms of killing are allowed in Hialeah destroys the contention that the prevention of killing animals is a compelling state interest. Further, if the concern here is for preventing cruelty to animals—possible pain and fear the sacrificial animals feel—the interest still does not rise to the level of "compelling." Again there is the problem that the city does not pursue this interest in many secular contexts: animals caught in traps surely must feel a significant amount of pain. . . .

As evidenced by the many religious groups that wrote an amicus [friend of the court] brief on behalf of the Church, it is believed that the outcome of *Church of the Lukumi* will have an impact far beyond the city of Hialeah. However, in all the commotion the case and the impact of *Smith* on "mainstream" religions, it must not be forgotten that it is the ancient sect of Santeria and religions like it that most need the protection of the U.S. Supreme Court. Smith offers up religions to the legislatures: it is the small, the unusual, even the unattractive religions and religious practices that will be hurt if the Court interprets *Smith* as requiring a victory for Hialeah.

The Free Exercise Clause, by its very terms and read in the light of its historic purposes, guarantees that believers of every faith, and not just the majority, are able to practice their religion without unnecessary interference from the government. The clause is not concerned with facial neutrality or general applicability. It singles out a particular category of human activities for particular protection, a protection that is most often needed by practitioners of non-mainsteam faiths who lack the ability to protect themselves in the political spheres.

"The only killing of animals deemed impermissible and unnecessary was that done for religious purposes."

Debate Centered on Whether Religious Discrimination or Public Health Was at Issue

David M. O'Brien

David M. O'Brien is a professor of political science at the University of Virginia. The following viewpoint is an excerpt from his book Animal Sacrifice and Religious Freedom. *In it, he describes a session of the U.S. Supreme Court in which lawyers on both sides presented their cases and were questioned by the justices. The attorney for the Church of the Lukumi Babalu Aye argued that the case was about discrimination against a minority religion. The attorney for the City of Hialeah, Florida, which had passed laws banning animal sacrifice, argued that these laws were necessary to prevent human health hazards and cruelty to animals. Because the laws did not prohibit other forms of animal killing and because there might have been less restrictive ways of controlling the disposal of dead animals, it was apparent that only the practice of religion was affected by them.*

Promptly at 10:00, the marshal of the Court announced the sitting of the justices with the traditional introduction: "Oyez! Oyez! Oyez! All persons having business before the Honorable, the Supreme Court of the United States, are ad-

David M. O'Brien, *Animal Sacrifice and Religious Freedom: Church of the Lukumi Babalu Aye v. City of Hialeah*. Lawrence, KS: University Press of Kansas, 2004.

monished to draw near and give their attention, for the Court is now sitting. God save the United States, and this Honorable Court."

In order of seniority, the justices filed into the courtroom from behind the curtains in back of the high bench. They took their seats, with the chief justice at the center and the associate justices on alternating sides, based on seniority. A minute later, Chief Justice [William] Rehnquist announced: "We'll hear argument first this morning in Number 91-948, *Church of the Lukumi Babalu Aye, Inc., v. the City of Hialeah.* Mr. Laycock."

Douglas Laycock rose from the table and went to the podium in front of the justices. . . .

In the time-honored tradition, Laycock began: "Mr. Chief Justice, may it please the Court." He immediately cut to what was at stake: "This is a case about open discrimination against a minority religion. The four ordinances challenged here were enacted in direct response to the church's announcement that it would build a church and practice [ritual animal sacrifice] in public. . . .

Justice [David] Souter asked if Laycock's argument was consistent with *Oregon v. Smith.* Laycock replied: "*Smith* says that religious acts are subject to neutral and generally applicable regulation, but *Smith* also reaffirms the long line of cases that says Government cannot resolve religious controversies. Government cannot decide whether sacrifice is necessary or unnecessary. An element of the offense under the State law is that the killing of the animal be unnecessary. That's also an element under three of the four ordinances. The only way to prove that sacrifice is unnecessary is to prove that Santeria is a false religion. To believers in Santeria, sacrifice is directly commanded by the gods in considerable detail on each occasion when it is required. To prove it unnecessary, you must prove the religion false, and when the prosecutor has to prove a religion false, the prosecutor is engaged in a heresy trial."

That response provoked a witty retort from the author of *Smith*. An irrepressible and acerbic questioner, Justice [Antonin] Scalia leaned forward to say: "Gee, I'm sure there are a lot of statutes, local, State and Federal, that use the term 'unnecessary.' Do you mean whenever somebody says that God tells him it is 'necessary,' that statute is invalid as applied to that person? That can't be right."

"The prohibition has to depend upon something other than the lack of necessity, Justice Scalia," Laycock continued. If Hialeah had a generally applicable prohibition on killing animals, the religious necessity of the practice would be irrelevant under *Smith*, but Hialeah's ordinances were not that, for they permitted the killing of animals for a whole range of reasons that the city considered necessary. Bow and arrow hunting was permissible, as was the extermination of rats and mice. The only killing of animals deemed impermissible and unnecessary was that done for religious purposes.

Chief Justice Rehnquist, whose dry sense of humor often draws laughter, asked straight-faced, "Is there a lot of bow and arrow hunting in the City of Hialeah?"

"Well, there is bow and arrow hunting by citizens of Hialeah who bring their kill, bring the entire carcass back to the city," Laycock replied. "There are farms in the City of Hialeah. There are veterinary offices that kill animals in Hialeah." . . .

The Law Was Not Generally Applicable

Justice Scalia [asked,] "Was there a finding that there was an antagonism towards Santeria? Was there any attempt to suppress the religion as such?"

Animal sacrifice was central to the Church of the Lukumi, Laycock argued. "When you suppress the central ritual, I think you suppress the religion."

Nevertheless, Justice Scalia reasoned perversely: "There have been people like, say, the Thugs were a religious group, I believe, and their central ritual was killing other people. Surely that can be suppressed." Of course, responded Laycock, but only under neutral and generally applicable laws against murder. But Scalia objected: "Hialeah says they have a universal, generally applicable law against ritualistic killing of animals." Laycock continued to try to explain that it was not a generally applicable law.

"No," Justice Scalia shot back. "Anybody who wants to have a ritual and—you're quite right, it doesn't happen very often in fraternities, though I imagine it happens now and then. But why isn't that a valid argument, that—they don't care whether you're doing it for religious reasons or not. They really don't care what your reason is."

Standing firm, Laycock responded sarcastically. "If that's a valid argument, you really have repealed the free exercise clause. Any lawyer in the country with that standard of drafting can draft an ordinance to get any church that happens to be at crosswise with the city council."

At that, Justice Souter came to his defense. "In effect you're saying you've got to define the act without reference to the intention of the people who perform the act." . . .

Asked by the justice where he faulted the lower court, Laycock stressed that Hialeah's ordinances had "nothing to do with the pain to the animals or the problem of disposal. There is no effort to insist that the compelling interest be pursued in a neutral or generally applicable way. There is no insistence that the interest be especially important. What all of these interests are incremental reductions in quite general problems that the city manages for secular purposes. We have carcasses lying on the road when pets are killed by cars. The city doesn't ban cars and it doesn't ban pets. It responds to the problem. An incremental reduction in a general problem cannot be obtained at the expense of the First Amendment."

Chief Justice Rehnquist now interrupted to inquire whether the city could distinguish between the accidental killing of pets and the intentional killing of animals. It could, said Laycock, quickly adding, "but the accident-intention distinction doesn't go to the disposal problem." The disposal problem involved only a small fraction of all the animals sacrificed. Hialeah's ordinances swept too broadly in banning all ritual animal sacrifice.

The chief justice nevertheless insisted that the distinction between accidental and intentional killing had a bearing on the disposal problem. Laycock held firm in countering that "most of the people who intentionally sacrifice do not improperly dispose of the animal. The finding is most of the sacrificed animals are eaten." . . .

"No killings of animals are included except the religious killings of animals, so it's under-inclusive in a sense, but they really have singled out religion for a prohibition that is applied nowhere else." With that, Laycock concluded: "If there are no further questions, I'll reserve my remaining time."

"Very well, Mr. Laycock," said Chief Justice Rehnquist. "Mr. Garrett, we'll hear from you."

Animal Sacrifice a Human Health Hazard

"Mr. Chief Justice and may it please the Court." [Richard] Garrett immediately launched into a discussion of the problems prompting the enactment of the ordinances. . . .

> I think that the record should reflect very clearly that Hialeah was responding to the problem of ritualistic sacrifices taking place in the city. What type of problems are we talking about? We're talking about human health hazards. The human health hazard evidence was evidence concerning the fact that when sacrifices take place, that as many as 52 animals in a single day are killed, and they are killed in a private residence in many instances and then they are decapitated, blood is put into pots, the animals are then often times left out in public places if there is a ritual that requires the animal to be left in a public place. There are problems connected with disease. The disease problems were

> discussed directly at the trial court as being a problem associated with the fact that the killings take place in residences, and as a result of that you have spilled blood, you have animal parts left in and around houses. That is different than the general problem of garbage.

Breaking into his argument, Justice [Sandra Day] O'Connor wondered whether it would have been possible for the city to approach the problem by adopting regulations specifying how animals may be killed and how to dispose of their carcasses.

"We believe not," Garrett said, and explained. . . .

> Assuming that you did enact a large number of ordinances, it's our position that they would be back in court saying you've in effect prohibited us from doing what we need to do in our religion, because now you have told us how we have to hold our knives, how we have to kill them, how we have to handle the blood in the particular ceremonies, and how we have to dispose of the animals, and our gods say that's not what we can do, and therefore we would have the same problem. We'd be back here with a different type of argument, but with the same kind of argument that the regulatory framework that we had created effectively precluded them from practicing their religion, and that is the problem that the city was facing.

Garrett's long argument was finally cut into by the chief: "You might have an ordinance that was easier to defend, though, in that situation, if it had been directed more precisely at the results of these proceedings rather than at the proceedings themselves."

Garrett replied that the ordinances did not target religion. They were, in fact, neutral with respect to religion. But before long, Justice Scalia cut him off. Playing the devil's advocate, he said: "You don't address the problems of hunters who kill animals cruelly, or dispose of their carcasses in a manner that you don't approve of or that's unsanitary, but you do pick upon this religious practice."

"Your Honor," Garrett explained, "there are two responses to that: This is not only a religious practice. There is evidence in the record which has not been mentioned that groups engage in this activity—malevolent magic is mentioned by one of their witnesses to describe what existed with respect to a goat that was cut in half and found on Miami Beach. There are also—there's also evidence in the record with respect to the fact that this particular type of practice is engaged in by Satanists, by witchcraft, voodoo, and this Court has never gone so far as to particularly extend protection to those groups." . . .

The City Allows Other Forms of Animal Killing

"Does the City of Hialeah allow people in their homes to trap mice and rats?" Justice O'Connor wondered aloud. "And to boil live lobsters and eat them?" In asking that question, the justice brought levity back into the courtroom. Laughter almost drowned out Garrett's feeble reply. "There is clearly a prohibition in the ordinances about the boiling of lobsters, if you read the ordinances as saying, as I think they do—or any other animals, so I don't believe that the lobsters. . ."

Again drawing laughter, Justice O'Connor continued: "You can't boil the lobster? You can't eat lobster? In Hialeah?" Caught off guard, Garrett said: "I think that technically—a technical reading of the ordinance would say that the boiling of lobsters is claused [*sic*] by, other animals. In your house, I think there is an exception."

"And what's the exception for the mice and rats?" Justice O'Connor tersely shot back. "Where do I find that?" At that point, Jeanne Baker [who had assisted with the brief] passed Laycock a note: "We've won." . . .

"Well," Justice [Anthony] Kennedy said with some exasperation, "if a church finds a slaughterhouse that is properly zoned and if it follows standards of applicability that are general for the disposal of animals, does it have a constitutional right to engage in its sacrificial services?"

No, reasserted Garrett, "we do not believe that a church would have a right to engage in animal sacrifice under circumstances that you have now described." Why? "Because we believe that the Constitution does not allow all religious practices to be engaged in even if they are central to the religion. The *Reynolds* case made it very clear that even though polygamy was central to the Mormon Church, that laws basically outlawing the polygamists' activities were laws that were constitutional. We would submit that the fact that it is important to a religion, if there is a legitimate governmental purpose to the particular restrictions. . . ."

Justice Kennedy again interrupted him: "Then is the legitimate governmental purpose here the prohibition of sacrifice, per se?"

Garrett replied: "We submit that it is. We submit that animal sacrifice is an appropriate category to be specifically focused on by a series of. . . ."

Before he could finish, however, Justice Kennedy again stopped him: "And is it a fair reading of these ordinances to find that that policy is implicit in these ordinances?"

"I think it is a fair reading of the ordinances," Garrett responded. "They in effect attempt to preclude animal sacrifice, and they do that in a number of different ways, and I think that is the question that the Court is facing, whether or not the attempt, and in this case a successful attempt to preclude the animal sacrifice as a governmental problem, is one that can be done under the First Amendment, free exercise provision."

"But would you not agree," Justice Kennedy interjected, "that in order for the prohibition to be legitimate, the public values that you assert are being furthered by the prohibition must not be allowed to be compromised through other exceptions to the killing that you allow, because otherwise you would have nothing left but an antagonism towards the religion. You do not like sacrifice to be done. If you have other values—cruelty to animals or public sanitation or whatever else—at least the other exceptions that you make from your general prohibition cannot permit those things to happen." . . .

"Mr. Garrett," Justice [John Paul] Stevens now interrupted, "the [district] court found specific harms to the animals. They were cruel in the way they did it and there were some disposal problems and certain other specific problems that they found. . . . Supposing there was one branch of the religion that required as a part of the ceremony that it be conducted in a slaughterhouse as Justice Kennedy suggests, that it dispose of the remains in a lawful manner, and that it had none of the side effects that trouble you, and very properly. But you have a religion that does sacrifice animals. Now, that religion would be prohibited by your ordinance even if none of the side effects occurred, or were permitted to occur by the religion, is that not correct?"

"That's correct. That would be an incidental impact of the ordinance, and we believe that that would be constitutional under *Smith*," Garrett responded, only to be cut off again by Justice Stevens. Drawing still more laughter, the justice observed: "The other thing that puzzles me, on the one hand you say there are tens of thousands of these sacrifices going on regularly and that's what prompted the ordinance, and then you say, as one very dramatic example of a goat being found on the beach that was apparently very unattractive and unhealthful. . . . But if that happens only once when there are thousands and thousands of sacrifices, which way does the example cut?"

Garrett stumbled, caught off guard by the examples, prompting more questions from Justice Stevens and more laughter in the courtroom over why littering statutes were not sufficient to address the problem of discarded animal carcasses.

There were such statutes, conceded Garrett, but they were ineffective. "They were obviously not accomplishing the purpose for which they were enacted, because it's very difficult to police a situation where people go out at night time or early in the morning with whole animals and leave them in parks, leave them under palm trees as it's dictated under the religious tenets, leave them at railroad crossings, leave them at the steps of courthouses in some instances—all of these dispersal of animal problems are problems that are in the record, and they are not simply a single goat."

A few more quick questions exhausted his remaining minutes, and Chief Justice Rehnquist stated blandly, "Thank you, Mr. Garrett."

The Church Complies with Humane Slaughter Regulations

Laycock had only four minutes for rebuttal, but Justice Scalia immediately cut in. "Do you agree, Mr. Laycock, that the limited slaughter that is allowed can only be allowed in a slaughterhouse?"

"That is not correct," countered Laycock:

> It can only be allowed where properly zoned. . . . Now, my clients have always been willing to accept regulation of the farms and *botanicas* [stores that sell religious items] which are not protected by the First Amendment. They're willing to accept reasonable zoning on the church itself. They are not willing to give up the rights of their members to sacrifice on special occasions such as births and weddings in the homes, but the church itself can be reasonably zoned, they're willing to comply with disposal regulations, but none of that would satisfy the city.

"How about humane slaughter regulations?" asked Chief Justice Rehnquist, prompting Laycock to respond: "We believe that we are in compliance with humane slaughter. There is a neutral prohibition on torture and torment that is not challenged."

"Why not?" interjected Justice Scalia. "Why not? Why shouldn't you be able to slaughter any way you want—humane or inhumane? If the theory of your case is correct, why—you know, why not go all the way?"

"Well," Laycock said, obviously exasperated, "because we're not tormenting and we're not torturing, we don't have to go all the way. I may be back some year with a different client who does." After the laughter died down, he continued: "The testimony is the method of sacrifice is very quick, except when it fails. The trial judge said it is somewhat unreliable and therefore it is cruel. There is no finding of how often it is unreliable, how often it misses. Those who are experienced in the method said they believe they don't miss, but the intended method of sacrifice is not cruel."

However, Chief Justice Rehnquist wondered: "If the intended method is not cruel, could not the city take into account that the intention just wasn't fulfilled sometimes and it turned out to be cruel in fact?"

"Perhaps they could take that into account in a neutral and generally applicable way," granted Laycock, "but again, look at all the other methods of killing which they permit with no regulation whatever, with no claim that they might be—that they have to be always instantaneous and never a mistake. No human activity has never been a mistake. I can put poison out in my yard in Hialeah and they don't tell me what kind. They don't say it has to be a quick-acting poison. The animal can wander off and suffer for a week, and that's okay with the city. That's expressly authorized in ordinance 87–40. It's only the religion that has to be perfect if it is to exist at all inside the city."

Before Laycock could conclude, time ran out at 11:01. Chief Justice Rehnquist thanked him, and the justices turned to the next case. . . . Outside on the steps of the Supreme Court building, Steven McFarland of the Christian Legal Society told reporters: "Anyone in Florida can kill an animal for sport, food, convenience or profit, but not for an exercise of religious worship. This discrimination against religion threatens every believer." Sam Rabinove, legal director of the American Jewish Committee, agreed. A ruling in favor of Hialeah would be "perilous for Jews. States could pass laws regulating kosher slaughter and prohibiting circumcision except when performed by a licensed physician. I'm not saying this will happen, but we would have no protection."

"If animal rights activists want to prevent such killings, they should fight to change generally applicable legal standards rather than standards enforced only against religious minorities."

The Court's Opinion Reinforced the Principle of Equal Protection for All

R. Ted Cruz

R. Ted Cruz is now the solictor general of the State of Texas and teaches U.S. Supreme Court litigation at the University of Texas School of Law. At the time he wrote the following viewpoint he was a student at Harvard Law School, where he was a founding editor of the Harvard Latino Law Review. *In his article he states that the Supreme Court was right to strike down the City of Hialeah's law against animal sacrifice because that law was intended to suppress only a religious practice and did not apply to people who killed animals for other reasons. The Court was also right, Cruz maintains, to base its decision on the principle of equal protection under the law, rather than on the "due process" criteria traditionally used to decide religious liberty cases, which have a more debatable legal foundation.*

In the aftermath of *Employment Division v. Smith*, countless scholars, practitioners, and interest groups decried the Supreme Court's holding that neutral and generally applicable laws incidentally restricting religion need not be justified by a

R. Ted Cruz, "Animal Sacrifice and Equal Protection Free Exercise," *Harvard Journal of Law & Public Policy*, Vol. 17, Winter, 1994. Reproduced by permission.

compelling state interest. Critics fervently awaited the next time the Court would consider a free exercise claim, hoping that the Court would clarify the *Smith* rule or, preferably, abandon it. Last Term, in *Church of the Lukumi Babalu Aye, Inc. v. City of Hialeah*, the Court addressed such a claim, considering an archetypal instance of a non-neutral, non-generally applicable regulation: a Florida city's ordinances directed at stopping animal sacrifice by practitioners of the Santeria religion. Rather than modifying or abandoning *Smith*, the Court utilized the *Smith* test to strike down the laws as violative of free exercise.

This holding, on its facts, was absolutely correct, as was the Court's continued reliance on *Smith*. It reflects, implicitly at least, a shift in free exercise doctrine from the vagaries of its substantive due process origins to a new-found reliance on equal protection as the proper source of incorporation. This reorientation of free exercise as applied to the states should be made explicit because equal protection provides a sounder and more textually supported genesis for free exercise incorporation.

Petitioner Ernesto Pichardo is a Santeria priest residing in Hialeah, Florida, who sought to bring the religion out into the open and to establish the Church of the Lukumi Babalu Aye as a visible and safe haven for the practice of Santeria. In response to Pichardo's public announcement of his intent to open a Santeria church practicing animal sacrifice, the City Council of Hialeah passed a series of ordinances outlawing animal "sacrifice" performed "in a public or private ritual or ceremony," while allowing hunting and fishing for sport, ordinary slaughter for food, experimentation for medical science, euthanasia of unhealty, unwanted, or commercially-valueless animals, and even use of live rabbits to train greyhounds. . . .

The Court's final result was absolutely correct, and the decision's unanimity sharply underscores the strength of its substantive conclusion. The ordinances, which were directly aimed at stopping Santeria, were violative of free exercise. Their fundamental flaw parallels that described by [philosopher John] Locke in 1689: "What may be spent on a Feast, may be spent on a Sacrifice." The conduct prohibited was prohibited in religious contexts only; the activity itself was legal except for the religious belief.

A Hypothetical Example

A simple hypothetical illustrates the ordinances' problems. Imagine two neighbors, Romulus and Remus. One day, Remus goes into his backyard and, for no reason whatsoever, grabs his pet chicken and slits its throat. He drops the carcass, turns around, and goes inside. Simultaneously, Romulus is in his backyard with his chicken. Like Remus, he grabs the bird and, with the identical motion, cuts its throat. Romulus, however, believes that his god cares about his dead poultry. Although their actions were identical, Romulus violated the Hialeah ordinances while Remus did not. The only difference is their motivations. Because the Hialeah ordinances differentiated among identical actions solely on the basis of religious belief, they did not regulate conduct; rather, they prohibited belief.

The interests asserted in defense of the ordinances were mere charades. Animal rights, enforced only against religious practitioners, are merely a pretense for suppressing religion. Outside a religious context, slitting the neck of an animal is not cruel or illegal in Hialeah. If animal rights activists want to prevent such killings, they should fight to change generally applicable legal standards rather than standards enforced only against religious minorities. Until the state is willing to regulate Remus, animal rights groups have no claim against Romulus alone. The interests in public safety are also facades. Both Romulus and Remus must now dispose of their dead chickens. If improper disposal is the problem, the state can regulate disposal rather than banning sacrifice altogether.

The Court Was Right to Rely on *Smith*

Not only was the Court's substantive conclusion correct; so was its reliance upon *Smith*, a rule that embodies the second half of Locke's analysis: "the Commonwealth . . . may forbid all [its] Subjects to kill any Calves . . . [because then] the law is not made about a religious, but a political matter." More importantly, *Smith* also reflects a reorientation in free exercise doctrine from substantive due process to equal protection as the proper source of incorporation. . . .

The *Smith* rule much more accurately follows the letter and spirit of the Constitution than did the prior, broader interpretation. . . .

If the validity of free exercise incorporation hinges on the soundness of substantive due process, then free exercise incorporation is in a precarious position indeed. . . . Equal protection, on the other hand, is quite promising. A law prohibiting conduct by some while allowing identical conduct by others can hardly be called equal; nor can a law expressly targeting a particular religious group for persecution. "Equal protection of the laws" envisions laws applying to everybody—generally applicable—and targeting nobody—neutral. Suddenly *Smith* reemerges. The rule in *Smith*, decried by Justice [Harry] Blackmun as "no more than an antidiscrimination principle," is just that—a rule of antidiscrimination embodying the principle of equal protection.

To the extent that substantive due process is an illegitimate doctrine (and that is another debate), so then is free exercise incorporation via due process. Equal protection, however, provides the solution. It necessitates some protection of free exercise (unlike due process), and suggests the very rule in *Smith*. The substantive result of *Lukumi Babalu Aye*, when framed in terms of equal protection, was obviously correct. Hialeah prohibited some from engaging in what all others could do, solely on the basis of religious belief. Equal protection also explains the use of *Smith* in *Lukumi Babalu Aye*. The Equal Protection

Clause illustrates (i) descriptively, what the Court was doing in *Smith*, and (ii) normatively, why the Court was doing it.

Chapter 3

Balancing Religious Liberty Against Effective Management of Prisons

Chapter Preface

Case Overview: *Cutter et al. v. Wilkinson, Director, Ohio Department of Correction, et al.* (2005)

In 2002 several inmates and former inmates of Ohio prisons filed suit, saying that they had been discriminated against in prison because they belonged to minority religions. Prison officials had denied them access to religious literature, denied them the opportunities for group worship that were granted to adherents of mainstream religions, failed to provide them with chaplains, forbidden them to dress according to the mandates of their religions, and withheld religious ceremonial items comparable to those adherents of mainstream religions were permitted.

Plaintiffs in the case were members of what the court described as non-mainstream religions. One of them was a Wiccan. (Wicca is a fast-growing neopagan religion that emphasizes the worship of nature. Though Wiccans often use the term *witchcraft*, it does not have the same meaning in their religion as it does to the general public.) Several plaintiffs were members of the small sect Asatru, which is based on ancient Norse religions. The other two belonged to tiny sects not likely to gain public support: one was a satanist and the other a minister of the Church of Jesus Christ Christian, which has ties to the white supremacist organization Aryan Nation. It had been determined, however, that theirs were bona fide religions and that their beliefs were sincere. Furthermore, the problems of these prisoners were not unique to members of small religions. Jews, Muslims, and even Catholics often are denied opportunity to observe all the requirements of their religions in prison.

It might seem obvious that this case did involve discrimination against minorities. That, however, was not the central point at issue. Previously, the U.S. Congress had passed the Religious Freedom Restoration Act (RFRA) in response to an unpopular U.S. Supreme Court ruling (*Employment Division v. Smith*) that had the effect of making it harder for religious exemptions to general rules to be obtained. The RFRA itself was found unconstitutional with respect to the states, though not with respect to federal law, because for technical reasons Congress lacked the authority to enact all the act's provisions. So Congress tried again, and unanimously passed a law narrower in scope, the Religious Land Use and Institutionalized Persons Act (RLUIPA). Among other things, RLUIPA states, "No government shall impose a substantial burden on the religious exercise of a person residing in or confined to an institution," unless the burden furthers "a compelling governmental interest," and does so by "the least restrictive means." This is clearly in accord with the free exercise clause of the First Amendment to the Constitution. Some people, however, felt that it violated the First Amendment's other clause—the establishment clause—by giving special privileges to religion. That was the position taken by the Ohio Department of Rehabilitation and Correction.

In 2003 the U.S. Court of Appeals for the Sixth Circuit, overruling a lower court decision in favor of the prisoners, declared that RLUIPA is unconstitutional because it "has the effect of impermissibly advancing religion by giving greater protection to religious rights than to other constitutionally protected rights." The law "also has the effect of encouraging prisoners to become religious in order to enjoy greater rights," wrote the circuit court judge. "One effect of RLUIPA is to induce prisoners to adopt or feign religious belief in order to receive the statute's benefits."

So what the Supreme Court had to decide was whether RLUIPA was constitutional. This was an important decision affecting much more than the rights of prisoners, because if the Court had ruled that the government cannot make laws protecting religious rights, then many other laws involving religious exemptions would have become invalid. Therefore, large religious groups as well as small ones were happy when, in 2005, it upheld the constitutionality of RLUIPA, saying that religious accommodations must be made for prisoners of all faiths except where such accommodations would interfere with prison security.

"We find RLUIPA's institutionalized-persons provision compatible with the Establishment Clause because it alleviates exceptional government-created burdens on private religious exercise."

The Court's Decision: There Is No Valid Reason to Deny the Practice of Non-Mainstream Religions in Prisons

Ruth Bader Ginsburg

Ruth Bader Ginsburg is a justice of the U.S. Supreme Court. The following viewpoint is the opinion she delivered representing the unanimous Court decision on the Cutter v. Wilkinson *case. Members of several small minority religions sued the state of Ohio under the Religious Land Use and Institutionalized Persons Act (RLUIPA) because they were not allowed to practice them in prison. The state argued that RLUIPA was unconstitutional because it violated the establishment clause of the First Amendment, which prohibits the government from making laws that establish religion. Justice Ginsburg points out, however, that removing government-imposed barriers to the practice of religion is an accommodation of their right to free exercise of their religion, not a government endorsement of religion. If such accommodation of religion were unconstitutional, then no provisions for traditionally recognized religions, such as permission for wor-*

Ruth Bader Ginsburg, unanimous opinion, *Cutter et al. v. Wilkinson, Director, Ohio Department of Rehabilitation and Correction, et al.*, U.S. Supreme Court, May 31, 2005.

ship services and the provision of chaplains, could be made either. Moreover, there is no reason to believe that it is impossible to apply RLUIPA without compromising prison security.

Section 3 of the Religious Land Use and Institutionalized Persons Act of 2000 (RLUIPA), provides in part: "No government shall impose a substantial burden on the religious exercise of a person residing in or confined to an institution," unless the burden furthers "a compelling governmental interest," and does so by "the least restrictive means." Plaintiffs below, petitioners here, are current and former inmates of institutions operated by the Ohio Department of Rehabilitation and Correction and assert that they are adherents of "nonmainstream" religions: the Satanist, Wicca, and Asatru religions, and the Church of Jesus Christ Christian. They complain that Ohio prison officials (respondents here), in violation of RLUIPA, have failed to accommodate their religious exercise

> In a variety of different ways, including retaliating and discriminating against them for exercising their nontraditional faiths, denying them access to religious literature, denying them the same opportunities for group worship that are granted to adherents of mainstream religions, forbidding them to adhere to the dress and appearance mandates of their religions, withholding religious ceremonial items that are substantially identical to those that the adherents of mainstream religions are permitted, and failing to provide a chaplain trained in their faith.

For purposes of this litigation at its current stage, respondents have stipulated that petitioners are members of bona fide religions and that they are sincere in their beliefs.

In response to petitioners' complaints, respondent prison officials have mounted a facial challenge to the institutionalized-persons provision of RLUIPA; respondents contend, *inter alia* [among other things], that the Act improperly advances religion in violation of the First Amendment's Establishment Clause. The District Court denied respondents' motion to dismiss petitioners' complaints, but the Court of Appeals reversed that determination. The appeals court held, as the prison officials urged, that the portion of RLUIPA applicable to institutionalized persons violates the Establishment Clause. We reverse the Court of Appeals' judgment.

"This Court has long recognized that the government may ... accommodate religious practices ... without violating the Establishment Clause." *Hobbie v. Unemployment Appeals Comm'n of Fla.* Just last Term, in *Locke v. Davey*, the Court reaffirmed that "there is room for play in the joints between" the Free Exercise and Establishment Clauses, allowing the government to accommodate religion beyond free exercise requirements, without offense to the Establishment Clause.... Section 3 of RLUIPA, we hold, does not, on its face, exceed the limits of permissible government accommodation of religious practices.

The History of RLUIPA

RLUIPA is the latest of long-running congressional efforts to accord religious exercise heightened protection from government-imposed burdens, consistent with this Court's precedents. Ten years before RLUIPA's enactment, the Court held, in *Employment Div., Dept. of Human Resources of Ore. v. Smith*, (1990), that the First Amendment's Free Exercise Clause does not inhibit enforcement of otherwise valid laws of general application that incidentally burden religious conduct. In particular, we ruled that the Free Exercise Clause did not bar Oregon from enforcing its blanket ban on peyote possession with no allowance for sacramental use of the drug. Accordingly, the State could deny unemployment benefits to persons dismissed from their jobs because of their religiously inspired peyote use. The Court recognized, however, that the political branches could shield religious exercise through legislative accommodation, for example, by making an exception to proscriptive drug laws for sacramental peyote use.

Responding to *Smith*. Congress enacted the Religious Freedom Restoration Act of 1993 (RFRA). RFRA "prohibits 'government' from 'substantially burden[ing]' a person's exercise of religion even if the burden results from a rule of general applicability unless the government can demonstrate the burden '(1) is in furtherance of a compelling governmental interest; and (2) is the least restrictive means of furthering that compelling governmental interest.'" . . . In *City of Boerne*, this Court invalidated RFRA as applied to States and their subdivisions, holding that the Act exceeded Congress' remedial powers under the Fourteenth Amendment.

Congress again responded, this time by enacting RLUIPA. Less sweeping than RFRA, and invoking federal authority under the Spending and Commerce Clauses, RLUIPA targets two areas: Section 2 of the Act concerns land-use regulation, Section 3 relates to religious exercise by institutionalized persons. Section 3, at issue here, provides that "no [state or local] government shall impose a substantial burden on the religious exercise of a person residing in or confined to an institution," unless the government shows that the burden furthers "a compelling governmental interest" and does so by "the least restrictive means." The Act defines "religious exercise" to include "any exercise of religion, whether or not compelled by, or central to, a system of religious belief." Section 3 applies when "the substantial burden [on religious exercise] is imposed in a program or activity that receives Federal financial assistance," or "the substantial burden affects, or removal of that substantial burden would affect, commerce with foreign nations, among the several States, or with Indian tribes." "A person may assert a violation of [RLUIPA] as a claim or defense in a judicial proceeding and obtain appropriate relief against a government."

Before enacting Section 3, Congress documented, in hearings spanning three years, that "frivolous or arbitrary" barriers impeded institutionalized persons' religious exercise. ("Whether from indifference, ignorance, bigotry, or lack of resources, some institutions restrict religious liberty in egregious and unnecessary ways.") To secure redress for inmates who encountered undue barriers to their religious observances, Congress carried over from RFRA the "compelling governmental interest""least restrictive means" standard. Lawmakers anticipated, however, that courts entertaining complaints under Section 3 would accord "due deference to the experience and expertise of prison and jail administrators."

History of this Case

Petitioners initially filed suit against respondents asserting claims under the First and Fourteenth Amendments. After RLUIPA's enactment, petitioners amended their complaints to include claims under Section 3. Respondents moved to dismiss the statutory claims, arguing, *inter alia*, that Section 3 violates the Establishment Clause. The United States intervened in the District Court to defend RLUIPA's constitutionality.

Adopting the report and recommendation of the Magistrate Judge, the District Court rejected the argument that Section 3 conflicts with the Establishment Clause. As to the Act's impact on a prison's staff and general inmate population, the court stated that RLUIPA, "permits safety and security—which are undisputedly compelling state interests—outweigh an inmate's claim to a religious accommodation." On the thin record before it, the court declined to find, as respondents had urged, that enforcement of RLUIPA, inevitably, would compromise prison security. . . .

The Court of Appeals held that Section 3 of RLUIPA "impermissibly advanc[es] religion by giving greater protection to religious rights than to other constitutionally protected rights."

Affording "religious prisoners rights superior to those of non-religious prisoners," the court suggested, might "encourag[e] prisoners to become religious in order to enjoy greater rights." . . . We now reverse the judgment of the Court of Appeals for the Sixth Circuit.

What the Constitution Requires

The Religion Clauses of the First Amendment provide: "Congress shall make no law respecting an establishment of religion, or prohibiting the free exercise thereof." The first of the two Clauses, commonly called the Establishment Clause, commands a separation of church and state. The second, the Free Exercise Clause, requires government respect for, and noninterference with, the religious beliefs and practices of our Nation's people. While the two Clauses express complementary values, they often exert conflicting pressure.

Our decisions recognize that "there is room for play in the joints" between the Clauses, some space for legislative action neither compelled by the Free Exercise Clause nor prohibited by the Establishment Clause. In accord with the majority of Courts of Appeals that have ruled on the question, we hold that Section 3 of RLUIPA fits within the corridor between the Religion Clauses: On its face, the Act qualifies as a permissible legislative accommodation of religion that is not barred by the Establishment Clause.

Foremost, we find RLUIPA's institutionalized-persons provision compatible with the Establishment Clause because it alleviates exceptional government-created burdens on private religious exercise. Removal of government-imposed burdens on religious exercise is more likely to be perceived "as an accommodation of the exercise of religion rather than as a Government endorsement of religion" [*Amos*]. Furthermore, the Act on its face does not founder on shoals our prior decisions have identified: Properly applying RLUIPA, courts must take adequate account of the burdens a requested accommodation may impose on nonbeneficiaries; and they must be satisfied that the Act's prescriptions are and will be administered neutrally among different faiths.

Exercise of Religion Involves Physical Acts

"The 'exercise of religion' often involves not only belief and profession but the performance of . . . physical acts [such as] assembling with others for a worship service [or] participating in sacramental use of bread and wine. . . ." *Smith.* Section 3 covers state-run institutions—mental hospitals, prisons, and the like—in which the government exerts a degree of control unparalleled in civilian society and severely disabling to private religious exercise. ("Institutional residents' right to practice their faith is at the mercy of those running the institution.") RLUIPA thus protects institutionalized persons who are unable freely to attend to their religious needs and are therefore dependent on the government's permission and accommodation for exercise of their religion.

We note in this regard the Federal Government's accommodation of religious practice by members of the military. In *Goldman v. Weinberger*, we held that the Free Exercise Clause did not require the Air Force to exempt an Orthodox Jewish officer from uniform dress regulations so that he could wear a yarmulke indoors. In a military community, the Court observed, "there is simply not the same [individual] autonomy as there is in the larger civilian community." Congress responded to *Goldman* by prescribing that "a member of the armed forces may wear an item of religious apparel while wearing the uniform," unless "the wearing of the item would interfere with the performance [of] military duties [or] the item of apparel is not neat and conservative."

We do not read RLUIPA to elevate accommodation of religious observances over an institution's need to maintain order and safety. Our decisions indicate that an accommodation must be measured so that it does not override other significant interests. In *Caldor*, the Court struck down a Connecticut law that "arm[ed] Sabbath observers with an absolute and unqualified right not to work on whatever day they designate[d] as their Sabbath." We held the law invalid under the Establishment Clause because it "unyielding[ly] weigh[ted]" the interests of Sabbatarians "over all other interests."

We have no cause to believe that RLUIPA would not be applied in an appropriately balanced way, with particular sensitivity to security concerns. While the Act adopts a "compelling governmental interest" standard, "context matters" in the application of that standard. Lawmakers supporting RLUIPA were mindful of the urgency of discipline, order, safety, and security in penal institutions. They anticipated that courts would apply the Act's standard with "due deference to the experience and expertise of prison and jail administrators in establishing necessary regulations and procedures to maintain good order, security and discipline, consistent with consideration of costs and limited resources."

Finally, RLUIPA does not differentiate among bona fide faiths. In *Kiryas Joel*, we invalidated a state law that carved out a separate school district to serve exclusively a community of highly religious Jews, the Satmar Hasidim. We held that the law violated the Establishment Clause, in part because it "single[d] out a particular religious sect for special treatment." RLUIPA presents no such defect. It confers no privileged status on any particular religious sect, and singles out no bona fide faith for disadvantageous treatment.

The Lower Court Misinterpreted Precedents

The Sixth Circuit misread our precedents to require invalidation of RLUIPA as "impermissibly advancing religion by giving greater protection to religious rights than to other constitutionally protected rights." Our decision in *Amos* counsels otherwise. There, we upheld against an Establishment Clause challenge a provision exempting "religious organizations from

Title VII's prohibition against discrimination in employment on the basis of religion." . . .

Were the Court of Appeals' view the correct reading of our decisions, all manner of religious accommodations would fall. Congressional permission for members of the military to wear religious apparel while in uniform would fail, as would accommodations Ohio itself makes. Ohio could not, as it now does, accommodate "traditionally recognized" religions: The State provides inmates with chaplains "but not with publicists or political consultants," and allows "prisoners to assemble for worship, but not for political rallies." . . .

We see no reason to anticipate that abusive prisoner litigation will overburden the operations of state and local institutions. The procedures mandated by the Prison Litigation Reform Act of 1995, we note, are designed to inhibit frivolous filings.

Should inmate requests for religious accommodations become excessive, impose unjustified burdens on other institutionalized persons, or jeopardize the effective functioning of an institution, the facility would be free to resist the imposition.

> *"[RLUIPA] is a law respecting religion, but not one respecting an establishment of religion."*

Concurring Opinion: Accommodating Prisoners' Religious Practices Is Not Unconstitutional

Clarence Thomas

Clarence Thomas is a justice of the U.S. Supreme Court. The following viewpoint is his concurring opinion in the Cutter v. Wilkinson *case, in which the State of Ohio asserted that the Religious Land Use and Institutionalized Persons Act (RLUIPA) was unconstitutional because it dealt with religion. The Court ruled unanimously that RLUIPA is valid and its provisions for the religious practices of prison inmates must be observed. Justice Thomas, however, wrote a separate opinion elaborating on the constitutionality of the law. In, it, he explains what the framers of the Constitution meant by the words "an establishment of religion." They were not saying that Congress could not make any laws that mentioned religion, he states; they intended merely to prevent the government from establishing an official religion that people were required by law to accept and to pay taxes for.*

I join the opinion of the Court. I agree with the Court that the Religious Land Use and Institutionalized Persons Act of 2000 (RLUIPA) is constitutional under our modern Establishment Clause case law. I write to explain why a proper histori-

Clarence Thomas, concurring opinion, *Cutter et al. v. Wilkinson, Director, Ohio Department of Rehabilitation and Correction, et al.*, U.S. Supreme Court, May 31, 2005.

cal understanding of the Clause as a federalism provision leads to the same conclusion.

The Establishment Clause provides that "Congress shall make no law respecting an establishment of religion." As I have explained, an important function of the Clause was to "ma[ke] clear that Congress could not interfere with state establishments." *Elk Grove Unified School Dist. v. Newdow*, (opinion concurring in judgment). The Clause, then, "is best understood as a federalism provision" that "protects state establishments from federal interference." Ohio contends that this federalism understanding of the Clause prevents federal oversight of state choices within the "'play in the joints'" between the Free Exercise and Establishment Clauses. In other words, Ohio asserts that the Clause protects the States from federal interference with otherwise constitutionally permissible choices regarding religious policy. In Ohio's view, RLUIPA intrudes on such state policy choices and hence violates the Clause.

Ohio's vision of the range of protected state authority overreads the Clause. Ohio and its *amici* [friends of the court] contend that, even though "States can no longer establish preferred churches" because the Clause has been incorporated against the States through the Fourteenth Amendment "Congress is as unable as ever to contravene constitutionally permissible *State choices regarding religious policy*." (emphasis added). That is not what the Clause says. The Clause prohibits Congress from enacting legislation "respecting an *establishment* of religion" (emphasis added); it does not prohibit Congress from enacting legislation "respecting religion" or "taking cognizance of religion" [according to author Philip Hamburger (2002)]. At the founding, establishment involved "'coercion of religious orthodoxy and of financial support *by force of law and threat of penalty*,'" *Newdow*, (Thomas, J., concurring in judgment), including "'governmental preferences for *particular* religious faiths.'" In other words, establishment at the founding involved, for example, mandatory observance or mandatory payment of taxes supporting ministers. To proscribe Congress from making laws "respecting an establishment of religion," therefore, was to forbid legislation respecting coercive state establishments, not to preclude Congress from legislating on religion, generally.

Ohio Misinterpreted the Framers' Statements

History, at least that presented by Ohio, does not show that the Clause hermetically seals the Federal Government out of the field of religion. Ohio points to, among other things, the words of James Madison in defense of the Constitution at the Virginia Ratifying Convention: "There is not a shadow of right in the general government to intermeddle with religion. Its least interference with it would be a most flagrant usurpation." Ohio also relies on James Iredell's statement discussing the Religious Test Clause at the North Carolina Ratifying Convention:

> [Congress] certainly [has] no authority to interfere in the establishment of any religion whatsoever. . . . Is there any power given to Congress in matters of religion? Can they pass a single act to impair our religious liberties? If they could, it would be a just cause of alarm. . . . If any future Congress should pass an act concerning the religion of the country, it would be an act which they are not authorized to pass, by the Constitution, and which the people would not obey.

These quotations do not establish the Framers' beliefs about the scope of the Establishment Clause. Instead, they demonstrate only that some of the Framers may have believed that the National Government had no authority to legislate concerning religion, because no enumerated power gave it that authority. Ohio's Spending Clause and Commerce Clause challenges, therefore, may well have merit.

In any event, Ohio has not shown that the Establishment Clause codified Madison's or Iredell's view that the Federal Government could not legislate regarding religion. An *unenacted* version of the Clause, proposed in the House of Representatives, demonstrates the opposite. It provided that "Congress shall make no laws touching religion, or infringing the rights of conscience." The words ultimately adopted, "Congress shall make no law respecting an establishment of religion," "identified a position from which [Madison] had once sought to distinguish his own". Whatever he thought of those words, "he clearly did not mind language less severe than that which he had [previously] used." The version of the Clause finally adopted is narrower than Ohio claims.

Nor does the other historical evidence on which Ohio relies—[U.S. Supreme Court Justice] Joseph Story's *Commentaries on the Constitution* [1833] prove its theory. Leaving aside the problems with relying on this source as an indicator of the original understanding, it is unpersuasive in its own right. Justice Story did say that "the whole power over the subject of religion is left exclusively to the state governments, to be acted upon according to their own sense of justice, and the state constitutions." In context, however, his statement concerned only Congress' inability to legislate with respect to religious *establishment.* ("The real object of the amendment was . . . to prevent any national ecclesiastical establishment, which should give to an hierarchy the exclusive patronage of the national government"); ("It was deemed advisable to exclude from the national government all power to act upon the subject. . . . It was impossible, that there should not arise perpetual strife and perpetual jealousy on the subject of ecclesiastical ascendancy, if the national government were left free to create a religious establishment").

In short, the view that the Establishment Clause precludes Congress from legislating respecting religion lacks historical provenance, at least based on the history of which I am aware.

Even when enacting laws that bind the States pursuant to valid exercises of its enumerated powers, Congress need not observe strict separation between church and state, or steer clear of the subject of religion. It need only refrain from making laws "respecting an establishment of religion"; it must not interfere with a state establishment of religion. For example, Congress presumably could not require a State to establish a religion any more than it could preclude a State from establishing a religion.

RLUIPA Does Not Involve Establishment of Religion

On its face—the relevant inquiry, as this is a facial challenge—RLUIPA is not a law "respecting an establishment of religion." RLUIPA provides, as relevant: "No government shall impose a substantial burden on the religious exercise of a person residing in or confined to an institution, . . . even if the burden results from a rule of general applicability, unless the government demonstrates that imposition of the burden on that person," first, "further[s] a compelling governmental interest," and second, "is the least restrictive means of furthering that compelling governmental interest." This provision does not prohibit or interfere with state establishments, since no State has established (or constitutionally could establish, given an incorporated Clause) a religion. Nor does the provision require a State to establish a religion: It does not force a State to coerce religious observance or payment of taxes supporting clergy, or require a State to prefer one religious sect over another. It is a law respecting religion, but not one respecting an establishment of religion.

In addition, RLUIPA's text applies to all laws passed by state and local governments, including "rule[s] of general applicability," whether or not they concern an establishment of religion. State and local governments obviously have many laws that have nothing to do with religion, let alone establishments thereof. Numerous applications of RLUIPA therefore do not contravene the Establishment Clause, and a facial challenge based on the Clause must fail.

It also bears noting that Congress, pursuant to its Spending Clause authority, conditioned the States' receipt of federal funds on their compliance with RLUIPA. . . . RLUIPA may well exceed the spending power. Nonetheless, while Congress' condition stands, the States subject themselves to that condition by voluntarily accepting federal funds. The States' voluntary acceptance of Congress' condition undercuts Ohio's argument that Congress is encroaching on its turf.

"By striking down RLUIPA, the 6th Circuit turns the First Amendment on its head. Words intended to protect religious liberty are used to deny religious liberty."

The Rights of Prisoners Involve Principles That Guard Religious Freedom for Everyone

Charles C. Haynes

Charles C. Haynes is a senior scholar and director of education programs at the First Amendment Center, a nonprofit organization that works to preserve and protect First Amendment freedoms. In the following viewpoint he declares that the U.S. Supreme Court decision on the religious rights of prison inmates—which had not yet been made at the time he wrote this article—will be of great importance to the future of religious freedom in America. He states that the Religious Land Use and Institutionalized Persons Act (RLUIPA), which prohibits prison officials from imposing a substantial burden on the religious practices of inmates, does not violate the principle of church-state separation, as the court of appeals had ruled. If it did, Haynes argues, then government could not pass any law that accommodates free exercise of religion for anyone.

When the U.S. Supreme Court rules on two church, state issues this term, the Ten Commandments [the issue of whether they can be displayed on government property] will

Charles C. Haynes, "Does Accommodating Religious Practice Violate First Amendment?" *First Amendment Center*, October 31, 2004. Reproduced by permission.

get the headlines. But the outcome of a second conflict—a lawsuit brought by prison inmates in Ohio—may have far greater implications for the future of religious freedom in America.

Rousing public interest in the Ohio case, *Cutter v. Wilkinson*, isn't easy. Mention "prisoners' rights" and public reaction ranges from indifference to outright hostility. This is especially true in this case because the plaintiffs belong to unconventional religions such as Asatru (a polytheistic religion) and highly unsavory groups like Satanists. But once Americans get past the unpopular religious beliefs of the inmates, they'll see principles at stake that guard religious freedom for everyone.

First, a little background: The Ohio prisoners sued claiming they were denied access to religious literature and the opportunity to conduct worship services. They invoked the Religious Land Use and Institutionalized Persons Act (RLUIPA), passed by Congress in 2000. Under RLUIPA, prison officials can't impose a substantial burden on the religious practice of inmates unless there is a compelling reason to do so (such as security or discipline)—and there is no less-restrictive way to protect the state's interest except by placing the burden.

The state of Ohio moved to dismiss the RLUIPA claims of the prisoners on the grounds that the law was unconstitutional. Last year, a three-judge panel of the 6th U.S. Circuit Court of Appeals agreed with the state, ruling that RLUIPA violates the establishment clause of the First Amendment because it sends a message of endorsement of religion and encourages "prisoners to become religious in order to enjoy greater rights." Since other appellate courts have reached the opposite conclusion, the Supreme Court has agreed to decide if RLUIPA violates church-state separation.

The 6th Circuit Court's Decision Was Wrong

The decision by the 6th Circuit is wrong and dangerous. Here's why: RLUIPA has nothing to do with state establishment of religion, but everything to do with protecting the freedom to practice one's faith. Some of the most ardent defenders of the establishment clause agree. "This is a reasonable law," argues Barry Lynn of Americans United for Separation of Church and State, "that requires prisons to meet the religious needs of inmates while still respecting the security concerns of correctional institutions."

Notice that RLUIPA doesn't guarantee that prisoners easily win accommodations from prison officials. Only sincere religious practices that are substantially burdened are eligible for protection. And even then prisoners aren't automatically granted their requests. Security or other concerns may be grounds for denying even the most sincere religious claims.

RLUIPA merely gives prisoners the right to make a request for accommodation—and requires the state to take it seriously. But if the Supreme Court upholds the 6th Circuit, then prison officials will be able to deny the religious freedom of prisoners on a routine basis, even when there isn't a strong reason to do so. That isn't church-state separation—this is state control over religion.

Consider the broader implications of the 6th Circuit ruling: If the establishment clause is interpreted to mean that government can't accommodate our freedom to practice religion, then religious freedom doesn't mean very much in this country. Anthony Picarello, general counsel of the Becket Fund for Religious Liberty, puts it this way: "The issue in Cutter is much bigger than RLUIPA—it's about whether government can pass any law that specially accommodates religious exercise. The Court's decision will affect what are literally thousands of accommodations for religion only. . . . The accommodations range from the U.S. military's allowing Jews in the armed services to wear yarmulkes, to Ohio's own exemption of minors from underage drinking laws for religious purposes."

Take an example from public schools. Many schools routinely exempt Jews, Muslims and Sikh students from "no head covering" policies. Of course, educators may have legitimate reasons such as gang activity for banning head coverings.

But the establishment clause shouldn't be used to prohibit school administrators from accommodating students who must cover their heads for religious reasons. After all, a yarmulke isn't a baseball cap. Claims of conscience can and should be treated differently by government officials.

By striking down RLUIPA, the 6th Circuit turns the First Amendment on its head. Words intended to protect religious liberty are used to deny religious liberty. The 6th Circuit court got it wrong. The U.S. Supreme Court can now set it right.

"RLUIPA requires state-run institutions such as prisons and mental institutions to alleviate substantial burdens that they place on the free exercise of [religion by] inmates and patients."

Prison Inmates Now Have the Right to Reasonable Religious Accommodations

Jeremy Leaming

Jeremy Leaming is a communications associate for Americans United for Separation of Church and State. In the following viewpoint he discusses the impact of the U.S. Supreme Court's decision that the federal Religious Land Use and Institutionalized Persons Act (RLUIPA) is not unconstitutional. The State of Ohio, unwilling to provide the accommodations for religious minorities that RLUIPA requires, claimed that the act violates the separation of church and state merely by making specific provision for the practice of religion. Though the lawsuit specifically involved only individual members of several small, unpopular religions, the upholding of RLUIPA is expected to relieve the injustices also faced in prison by larger minorities, such as Jewish and Muslim inmates, who often are not allowed the same privileges as Christian inmates.

When Mitzi Hamilton, a low-level offender, entered Virginia corrections officials' custody in 2003 she made what she thought was a simple request—a kosher diet to ad-

Jeremy Leaming, "Conscience Clause," *Church & State*, July-August 2005.

here to the dictates of her Jewish faith. Hamilton, 36, was sentenced to five-and-a-half years behind bars for fraud and forgery and, like many of her fellow inmates, was relying on her religious beliefs to help during incarceration. She quickly discovered, however, that inmates from minority faiths face serious obstacles. Virginia correctional officials responded to her request for a kosher diet by assigning her to a maximum-security prison in Troy, the only women's facility to offer meals intended to satisfy Jewish inmates' requests. Thus, in order to observe the tenets of her faith, Hamilton would have to do hard time with other prisoners identified as violent and dangerous. Hamilton's attorney Richard McKewen told *Church & State* that she and other Jewish prisoners have also had problems trying to gain access to a rabbi and permission to observe rituals of their religion.

Now, thanks to the U.S. Supreme Court, Hamilton and inmates like her have more legal clout for their religious liberty claims. In May [2005], the justices unanimously upheld a federal law guaranteeing prisoners the right to ask for reasonable religious accommodations. The Religious Land Use and Institutionalized Persons Act (RLUIPA), the court said, does not violate the First Amendment and must be obeyed.

Enacted during the [Bill] Clinton presidency, RLUIPA requires state-run institutions such as prisons and mental institutions to alleviate substantial burdens that they place on the free exercise of inmates and patients. Government officials may restrict religious observance only if they can prove that such restrictions further "a compelling governmental interest" and do so by "the least restrictive means." Some state correctional officials, however, have resisted the strictures of RLUIPA, and a number of conflicts have wound up in the federal courts. In one of those lawsuits, the 6th U.S. Circuit Court of Appeals agreed with Ohio correctional officials that RLUIPA violates the separation of church and state because it favors religious freedom over other fundamental rights.

RLUIPA Does Not Violate Separation of Church and State

In its May 31 *Cutter v. Wilkinson* decision, however, the Supreme Court concluded that the federal law does not "exceed the limits of permissible government accommodation of religious practices." In a tightly crafted opinion, Justice Ruth Bader Ginsburg found that Section 3 of RLUIPA does not subvert the First Amendment "because it alleviates exceptional government-created burdens on private religious exercise."

But Ginsburg made clear that the federal law does not "elevate accommodation of religious observances over" prison security needs. Indeed, Ginsburg noted that federal court precedent shows that "an accommodation must be measured so that it does not override other significant interests."

Ginsburg also suggested that RLUIPA's protection for prisoners' religious liberties would not be an impediment to maintaining the safety and security of other inmates. "We have no cause to believe," she wrote, "that RLUIPA would not be applied in an appropriately balanced way, with particular sensitivity to security concerns." In conclusion, Ginsburg added, "Should inmate requests for religious accommodations become excessive, impose unjustified burdens on other institutionalized persons, or jeopardize the effective functioning of an institution, the facility would be free to resist the imposition."

Law Students Worked on the Case

The *Cutter* case evolved from a number of religious liberty lawsuits lodged against the Ohio Department of Rehabilitation and Correction in the late 1990s. One inmate, a member of Asatru, a pre-Christian religion that reveres the Norse gods, was being represented by Ohio State University [OSU] Law School's Clinical Programs. David Goldberger, an OSU law professor and staff attorney in the school's Clinical Programs, told *Church & State* that he became involved in the case in late 1999.

After RLUlPA was passed in 2000, Goldberger and the Clinical Programs students amended their Ohio prisoner's complaint to include a claim that prison officials had violated the new federal statute. At the time, Goldberger said he had heard of the other prisoner lawsuits on religious liberty grounds and wanted to consolidate them into one action to show the "breadth of the problem" for minority religions.

A U.S. district judge agreed, and the lawsuit soon included an inmate trying to practice Wicca, a pre-Christian religion focusing on nature, a Satanist and an inmate belonging to the Church of Jesus Christ Christian, which calls for racial separation. The prisoners' combined legal effort argued that Ohio corrections officials had blocked them from practicing their religious beliefs in a number of ways, including denial of requests for literature and other accoutrements needed for their religious practices.

"The case was taken as pro bono [without charge]" Goldberger said, "providing students a rich educational experience. Over the years, there have been a slew of students working on this case."

Attorneys for Ohio state government responded by arguing that RLUIPA is unconstitutional and asked the U.S. district court to dismiss the complaint. The district judge refused, but in fall 2003 a three-judge panel of the 6th Circuit reversed, siding with Ohio corrections officials. Since a number of other federal circuits, including the 4th, 7th and 9th, had ruled that RLUIPA did not violate the First Amendment, it was hardly surprising that the Supreme Court would eventually step in to referee the disagreement.

Many Groups Supported RLUIPA

Goldberger said he thought that many advocacy groups would rather have seen a case at the high court from one of the other circuits, where "kinder, gentler plaintiffs" were represented. "I was also worried about our chances because of the plaintiffs," Goldberger said, "but these prisoners were our clients and we could not exactly quit at the twelfth hour. We had to proceed."

Goldberger thought his case was particularly attractive to the Supreme Court because the 6th Circuit's ruling dealt only with the First Amendment, not whether Congress had exceeded its Spending or Commerce Clause authorities in passing RLUIPA.

A wide range of public interest and advocacy organizations, some of whom are often on opposite sides of church-state debates, filed friend-of-the-court briefs with the Supreme Court arguing in favor of RLUIPA. Americans United for Separation of Church and State and the American Civil Liberties Union supposed the federal law, as did the socially conservative Becket Fund for Religious Liberty.

The alliance is hardly surprising. Many of these same groups joined forces to ask Congress to pass RLUIPA in the first place. The law is a successor to the 1993 federal Religious Freedom Restoration Act (RFRA), a federal statute that barred all government actions substantially burdensome to some religious freedoms, unless the government actions were supported by a compelling interest.

RFRA was spurred by the Supreme Court's 1990 ruling in *Employment Division v. Smith*. The *Smith* decision, authored by Justice Antonin Scalia, was immediately controversial. According to Scalia, "neutral laws" that burden minorities' religious freedom do not require much justification from the government. Before *Smith*, the high court had ruled that government-imposed burdens on religious freedom must be accompanied by a showing of strong public necessity. It was that test that Congress was intent on restoring.

But in 1997 in *City of Boerne v. Flores*, the high court invalidated RFRA as applied to the states, saying Congress had exceeded its constitutional power. Faced with this judicial hurdle, Congress tried again with RLUIPA. This measure targets only two areas of government regulation—those relating to land use and zoning and those dealing with institutionalized persons. (Congress grounded the federal act in its Spending and Commerce Clause powers.)

The high court's recent *Cutter* ruling only dealt with the section on institutionalized persons. In a footnote, Ginsburg said the justices were expressing "no view on the validity" of Section 2, the land-use portion of RLUIPA. (There are a number of federal cases dealing with the constitutionality of the land-use section of RLUIPA.)

Justice Clarence Thomas, in a rather tortuous concurring opinion, continued his crusade against long-standing precedents upholding church-state separation. He argued that the First Amendment's Establishment Clause is a "federalism provision" only meant to keep the federal government from interfering with state establishments of religion.

"Congress need not observe strict separation between church and state," asserted Thomas, "or steer clear of the subject of religion. It need only refrain from making laws 'respecting an establishment of religion'; it must not interfere with a state establishment of religion. "For example," Thomas continued, "Congress presumably could not require a State to establish a religion any more than it could preclude a State from establishing a religion."

Though RLUIPA did not violate the First Amendment, Thomas maintained in a footnote that the federal act "may well exceed Congress' authority under either the Spending Clause or the Commerce Clause." Yet in his concurring opinion, Thomas concluded that as long as RLUIPA stands, "the States subject themselves to that condition by voluntarily accepting federal funds. The States' voluntary acceptance of Congress' condition undercuts Ohio's argument that Congress is encroaching on its turf."

The Court's Decision Won Praise

It was Ginsburg's majority decision, however, that won praise from the ideologically diverse groups that had argued in favor of RLUIPA.

"This is a sensible decision that affirms the value of religious freedom while giving correctional institutions the ability to meet their security needs," said the Rev. Barry W. Lynn, Americans United executive director. "This decision reminds us that government must treat all religions equally. The state cannot play favorites among religions."

Goldberger, the lawyer for the Ohio inmates, told *Church & State* that he was pleased with Ginsburg's ruling. "I was comfortable with what the court did," he said, "I did not think there was a need for a sweeping ruling that would place religious needs over non-religious needs."

It's also good news for Mitzi Hamilton, the Jewish inmate in Virginia. McKewen, her attorney, was heartened, but not surprised by the high court's ruling as well. "I think it was a no-brainer, hence the 9–0 decision," he said. According to McKewen, Congress intended RLUIPA to help clients like his and those in *Cutter* overcome intentional or unintentional government-imposed burdens on their religious practices.

Hamilton has already made substantial progress. In 2003, McKewen filed a federal lawsuit on her behalf, charging Virginia officials with violating her religious liberty and citing RLUIPA and constitutional protections. Virginia corrections officials agreed to move Hamilton to a low-security facility and provide her kosher meals, thus settling a major issue in her lawsuit, but her attorney says the ruling in *Cutter* will prove useful in persuading the corrections officials to treat minority faiths on a par with majority ones.

"Hamilton had put in repeated requests to light one candle for Shabbat and prison officials turned her down," McKewen said. "It seems to me inequitable given that at Christmas-time services, officials allowed hundreds of candles to be lit and held by inmates."

Jewish and Muslim Inmates Are Treated Unjustly

McKewen said Virginia prison officials are still struggling in regard to the treatment of Jewish and Muslim inmates. For example, Hamilton and other prisoners continue to have a difficult time consulting rabbis. The Christian inmates, McKewen charges, have regular access to chaplains and are able to attend church-sponsored events at the prisons. For the Jewish inmates, however, the onus is on them to find a rabbi who will make a trip to the prison, which are often in rural areas where there is no synagogue nearby. The Jewish clergy must then go through security to meet with the inmates. "The rabbis are also required to go through background checks," McKewen said, "so there are several hurdles to overcome before they can visit the inmates."

Virginia officials also, according to McKewen, continue to deny Jewish inmates kosher Passover meals, which would include a traditional Seder plate, consisting typically of horseradish, a sprig of parsley, a vegetable, a small quantity of chopped apples and nuts, a bone and a hard boiled egg. The Seder plate is symbolic in nature and not meant to replace the kosher meal.

"We will continue to do whatever it takes to vindicate these inmates," said McKewen, who is a staff attorney with the Institute for Public Representation at the Georgetown University Law Center. "These are the kinds of injustices Congress had in mind when RLUIPA was passed. Look at the legislative history, which the majority cites in *Cutter* and you'll see that Congress has a federal policy on this issue, and if you take federal funds you'll have to comply with federal policy."

Justice Ginsburg noted in *Cutter* that congressional hearings found widespread indifference and hostility to minority prisoners' claims. The investigation, which spanned three years, found frivolous or arbitrary barriers impeding prisoners' religious liberties. In a footnote, Ginsburg included numerous passages from some of the hearings, revealing an array of requests for religious accommodations that state prison officials fought.

For example, a state prison in Ohio refused to provide Muslims with halal [ritually fit for use] food, while making kosher food available to Jewish inmates. In Michigan, prison officials barred the lighting of Hanukkah candles at all state prisons, but allowed smoking and the lighting of votive candles. A Catholic priest in Tulsa, Okla., told a House panel that he was in a constant battle with prison officials over the use of sacramental wine for mass, and that inmates' religious possessions "such as the Bible, the Koran, the Talmud or items needed by Native Americans . . . were frequently treated with contempt and were confiscated, damaged or discarded."

Now that RLUIPA has been upheld by the Supreme Court, some of the claims may have a different outcome.

"The RLUIPA is necessary to protect institutionalized persons who are dependent upon the government's permission and accommodation for the exercise of their religion."

The Supreme Court's Decision Was a Significant Victory for Minority Religions

Dana D. Eilers

Dana D. Eilers is a retired attorney, herself a pagan, who has written extensively about pagan religions and about the civil rights of pagans. She teaches and speaks on these subjects and is the author of several books. In the following viewpoint she explains why the Religious Land Use and Institutionalized Persons Act (RLUIPA) is important to pagans and other religious minorities, and why she believes the decision of the U.S. Supreme Court to uphold it will be a significant moment in the history of American jurisprudence. She warns, however, that prison security can still override religious freedom, and that pagans may still face inquiry as to whether their religious beliefs are sincere.

On May 31, 2005, the United States Supreme Court issued a decision in the case of *Cutter, et al. v. Wilkinson, et al.* which will be, for Pagans a significant moment in the history of American jurisprudence. In this case, Pagan plaintiffs have successfully mounted a constitutional challenge in the United States Supreme Court. The decision itself, however, only rules

Dana D. Eilers, "Analysis of *Cutter v. Wilkinson*: Supreme Court Rules in Favor of pagans," *Witches' Voice (www.witchvox.com)*, June 26, 2005. Reproduced by permission of the author.

on a narrow issue, which is whether the Religious Land Use and Institutionalized Persons Act of 2000 is constitutional when held up against the First Amendment of the federal Constitution. Before we all start jumping up and down, we need to examine the history of the Religious Land Use and Institutionalized Persons Act.

As noted by Justice Ruth Bader Ginsburg, who wrote the majority opinion in *Cutter*, there has been a long-running attempt by Congress to afford religious exercise some sort of increased protection from government-imposed burdens, which protection had to be consistent with the precedents established by the U.S. Supreme Court. In the Supreme Court decision of *Employment Div., Dept. of Human Resources of Oregon v. Smith*, the Supremes (that is, the United States Supreme Court), held that the state of Oregon could enforce a blanket ban on peyote possession without making any allowance for sacramental use of the drug. This ruling permitted Oregon to deny unemployment benefits to persons dismissed from employment because of religious or ritual peyote use. After the *Smith* case, Congress enacted the Religious Freedom Restoration Act of 1993 (RFRA) in an attempt to provide some sort of protection for religious exercise (such as that in the *Smith* case) from government interference. Unfortunately, the Supremes struck down the RFRA in the case of *City of Boerne v. Flores*, and found that Congress had exceeded its scope of power in enacting the RFRA.

Congress went back to the legislative drawing board and in 2000, enacted the Religious Land Use and Institutionalized Persons Act of 2000 (RLUIPA). It is Section 3 of this federal statute which came under fire in the *Cutter* case. Section 3 provides that "no [state or local] government shall impose a substantial burden on the religious exercise of a person residing in or confined to an institution," unless the government can show that the burden imposed furthers "a compelling governmental [interest]" and accomplishes that task by "the least restrictive means." Notably, Section 2 of the RLUIPA deals with land use regulation, but this particular section was not at issue in the *Cutter* case. Cases brought under Section 2 of the RLUIPA might involve Pagan Temples, Wiccan churches, etc. operating out of private homes in areas zoned for residential use.

The Case Involved Pagan Plaintiffs

For Pagans, the big hoopla surrounding *Cutter* is that the case involves identifiable Pagan plaintiffs/petitioners to the United States Supreme Court. The people who wound up in the Supreme Court were current and former prisoners in the Ohio Department of Rehabilitation and Correction. Collectively, they are described by Justice Ginsburg in as "adherents of 'nonmainstream' religions: the Satanist, Wicca, and Asatru religions, and the Church of Jesus Christ Christian." In looking at the history of *Cutter* before it got to the Supremes, we see that in the federal district court, there was a plaintiff J. Lee Hampton, who was Wiccan and a practicing witch; [and] there were Asatru plaintiffs. Interestingly, plaintiff Jon B. Cutter was a Satanist, and [another] plaintiff was a member and ordained minister of the Church of Jesus Christ Christian (CJCC), which had ties to the Aryan Nation. Certainly, the Satanist plaintiff and the CJCC plaintiff are not particularly sympathetic given the current mainstream notion that the United States is a "Christian nation."

It is important to note that from the get go, there was a concession from the defendants that the plaintiffs practiced bona fide religions, and that plaintiffs' beliefs were genuine. In the Supreme Court case, Judge Ginsburg stated that there was a stipulation regarding the plaintiffs/petitioners: they were members of bona fide religions and were sincere in their beliefs. So, there was no issue as to whether Wicca, the Asatru, Satanism, or the CJCC were religions meritorious of First Amendment protection. This had already been stipulated to by the defense. Arguably, a case might still arise in the Supreme Court which calls into question the validity, for First Amendment purposes, of these religions.

So, what brought these people to court in the first place? While incarcerated, the various plaintiffs/petitioners sought to practice their respective religions which were not "traditionally recognized by the Ohio Department of Rehabilitation and Corrections (ODRC)." While trying to practice their faiths in prison, they were allegedly subjected to illegal or unconstitutional treatment, including "denial of access to religious literature and/or items necessary to practice their religion . . . denial of the opportunity to conduct religious services . . . denial of the freedom to conform their dress or appearance to that required by their religion . . . denial of a prison chaplain specifically trained in and dedicated to their religion . . . and retaliation and discrimination by ODRC staff resulting from attempts to advance and practice their religion." Ultimately, the plaintiffs/petitioners amended their initial court pleadings to include assertions that the ODRC practices violated the RLUIPA. When this occurred, the defendants moved to dismiss the prisoners' actions on the grounds that the RLUIPA was unconstitutional, asserting that Section 3 of RLUIPA violated the Establishment Clause of the First Amendment.

The United States District Court for the Southern District of Ohio, Eastern Division, agreed with the plaintiff/petitioners and denied the defendants' motions to dismiss the prisoners' actions. The case was taken on interlocutory appeal to the Sixth Circuit federal court of appeals and on November 7, 2003, the federal appellate court reversed the district court. In essence, the federal appellate court came down on the side of the defendants. The plaintiffs/petitioners then filed a Writ of Certiorari [a request for review] with the United States Supreme Court seeking review of the federal appellate court decision. The stage was now set for this landmark constitutional challenge to be mounted by Pagans in the United States Supreme Court.

Pagans Are Not the Only Mistreated Religious Minority

Justice Ginsburg began by stating that government could accommodate religious practices without violating the Establishment Clause. She followed with this statement: "But Section 3 of RLUIPA . . . does not, on its face, exceed the limits of permissible government accommodation of religious practices." RLUIPA applies to entities which accept federal financial assistance, and it was noted that every state, including Ohio, accepts federal funding for its prisons. Justice Ginsburg also made reference to Congressional hearings regarding the abuse of prisoner religious freedoms. The *Cutter* decision is worth reading if only for the insight offered by the portions of the hearing transcripts which appear in the decision. Pagans often think of themselves as the only mistreated religious minority. In some prisons, there is considerable opposition to the Catholic use of Sacramental Wine. Other abuses are noted and are worth noting by everyone.

Judge Ginsburg's majority opinion reversed the decision of the Sixth Circuit Court of Appeals and specifically stated: ". . . we find RLUIPA's institutionalized-persons provision compatible with the Establishment Clause because it alleviates exceptional government-created burdens on private religious exercise." The Court reminded everyone that in state-run institutions such as mental hospitals and prisons, there is a degree of governmental control which is "unparalleled in civilian society and severely disabling to private religious exercise." In such a climate, the RLUIPA is necessary to protect institutionalized persons who are dependent upon the government's permission and accommodation for the exercise of their religion. However, before seeking recourse to the courts and RLU-

IPA, institutionalized persons must first exhaust their administrative remedies in accordance with the Prison Litigation Reform Act of 1995.

Once a RLUIPA claim reaches the court, there must be an adequate account of any burden which the requested accommodation may impose, and the RLUIPA must be administered neutrally among different faiths. No religious sect can have privileged status under the statute, and the statute does not single out any bona fide faith for disadvantageous treatment. However, prison security does represent a compelling state interest under RLUIPA, and deference to the expertise of institutional officials is due. Thus, prison officials may make inquiry as to whether the "religiosity" for which accommodation is requested is, in fact, authentic; the professed "religiosity" must be genuine.

So, we are still left with a judicial climate much as that before this case was decided. Prison security may well be the overriding issue; prisoners still have to exhaust their administrative remedies; and there will still be inquiry as to whether the belief and/or practice for which accommodation is sought is genuine and/or sincere. Incarcerated Pagans continue to be leaders in the fight for Pagan religious freedom, their cases providing us with significant legal clout in our struggle for recognition and equality.

Chapter 4

Balancing Religious Liberty Against Prohibition of Hallucinogenic Drugs

Chapter Preface

Case Overview: *Gonzales, Attorney General, et al. v. O Centro Espirita Beneficiente Uniao do Vegetal, et al.* (2006)

Can people who use hallucinogenic drugs in the practice of their religions be exempted from general laws prohibiting such drugs? The U.S. Supreme Court's decision in the well-known 1990 case of *Employment Division v. Smith*, in which employees were denied unemployment compensation after being fired for using peyote in a religious ceremony, said no. But after that decision, Congress passed the Religious Freedom Restoration Act (RFRA), which, though later found to be unconstitutional on technical grounds with respect to state and local laws, does apply to federal laws such as the Controlled Substances Act (CSA). Therefore, in 2006 the Supreme Court considered the question again.

O Centro Espirita Beneficiente Uniao do Vegetal (UDV) is a Brazilian-based Christian Spiritist sect that uses a hallucinogenic tea called *hoasca* (pronounced wass-ca) in its rituals. UDV has only a few members in the United States, who import the *hoasca* from Brazil. In 1999 federal agents raided UDV's office and seized a shipment. Its leader then sued the federal government under the RFRA. The church's claim that disallowing the use of *hoasca* would restrict members' religious freedom was not contested, but federal lawyers maintained that the government had a compelling interest (that is, a reason strong enough to override religious liberty) in protecting health and safety, preventing the diversion of *hoasca* to nonmembers, and complying with international treaties on drug traffic. Both the trial court and the court of appeals decided that those treaties did not cover *hoasca* and that the evidence presented by both sides on health risks and potential diversion was equally balanced, ruling that the government had failed to demonstrate a compelling interest.

In the Supreme Court's review of the case, the government asserted that the health risks of *hoasca*, and the chances of its use spreading beyond the church, were so great that the CSA must be enforced uniformly, without any exceptions. But the Court, in a unanimous decision, rejected this argument. It declared that the government had not offered any good reason why there could be no exceptions to the law, and that the intent of Congress in passing the RFRA was to require consideration of exceptions. Moreover, there was already an exception to the CSA. Native Americans who are members of federally recognized tribes are permitted to use the hallucinogenic drug peyote in religious ceremonies. The Court reasoned that since hundreds of thousands of them are doing so despite such drugs being dangerous and subject to abuse, that fact alone cannot justify denying the same right to the 130 members of UDV.

This decision is likely to have an impact on other cases where illegal drugs are used in religious rituals. It applies, however only to groups where such use is a traditional, integral part of the religion; it offers no support to new religions established simply to get around drug laws. Furthermore, different criteria would prevail in cases involving recreational drugs sought by large numbers of people. Despite the government's statement to the contrary, most people familiar with *hoasca* (also known as ayahuasca) do not believe it has potential to become a street drug. It has an unpleasant taste, and it induces not only hallucinations but severe vomiting. Journalist Peter Gorman, who has written extensively about its religious value and has attended ceremonies in Brazil where it is used, has said, "I'm not saying there isn't a kid out there who might try ayahuasca recreationally, but I'll bet you they won't try it twice."

The main significance of the *Uniao do Vegetal* decision lies in its implication for the future of religious liberty in general. For that reason, it was applauded by many large religious groups that do not themselves approve of drug use.

"The Government's argument echoes the classic rejoinder of bureaucrats throughout history: If I make an exception for you, I'll have to make one for everybody, so no exceptions."

The Court's Decision: The Government Has Not Demonstrated a Compelling Reason for Allowing No Exceptions to the Controlled Substances Act

John Roberts

John Roberts is the chief justice of the U.S. Supreme Court. The following viewpoint is an excerpt from the opinion he delivered in the case of Gonzales v. Uniao do Vegetal, *in which the Court ruled unanimously that religious exemption from laws against drug use cannot be denied on the grounds of uniform law enforcement. In it, he states that the Court found no good reason why exceptions cannot be made to the Controlled Substances Act, and that the Religious Freedom Restoration Act requires religious exemptions to law be allowed unless the government can demonstrate a compelling interest (an overriding need to protect the public) in applying them to everyone. Furthermore, he points out, there is already an exception to the drug law for Native American religions, and there is no justification for not granting the same right to others.*

John Roberts, unanimous opinion, *Gonzales, Attorney General, et al. v. O Centro Espirita Beneficiente Uniao do Vegetal et al.* U.S. Supreme Court, February 21, 2006.

O Centro Espirita Beneficiente Uniao do Vegetal (UDV) is a Christian Spiritist sect based in Brazil, with an American branch of approximately 130 individuals. Central to the UDV's faith is receiving communion through *hoasca* (pronounced "wass-ca"), a sacramental tea made from two plants unique to the Amazon region. One of the plants, *psychotria viridis*, contains dimethyltryptamine (DMT), a hallucinogen whose effects are enhanced by alkaloids from the other plant, *banisteriopsis caapi*. DMT, as well as "any material, compound, mixture, or preparation, which contains any quantity of [DMT]," is listed in Schedule I of the Controlled Substances Act.

In 1999, United States Customs inspectors intercepted a shipment to the American UDV containing three drums of *hoasca*. A subsequent investigation revealed that the UDV had received 14 prior shipments of *hoasca*. The inspectors seized the intercepted shipment and threatened the UDV with prosecution.

The UDV filed suit against the Attorney General and other federal law enforcement officials, seeking declaratory and injunctive relief. The complaint alleged, *inter alia* [among other things] that applying the Controlled Substances Act to the UDV's sacramental use of *hoasca* violates RFRA. Prior to trial, the UDV moved for a preliminary injunction, so that it could continue to practice its faith pending trial on the merits.

The District Court Ruling

At a hearing on the preliminary injunction, the Government conceded that the challenged application of the Controlled Substances Act would substantially burden a sincere exercise of religion by the UDV. The Government argued, however, that this burden did not violate RFRA [the Religious Freedom Restoration Act of 1993], because applying the Controlled Substances Act in this case was the least restrictive means of advancing three compelling governmental interests: protecting the health and safety of UDV members, preventing the diversion of *hoasca* from the church to recreational users, and complying with the 1971 United Nations Convention on Psychotropic Substances, a treaty signed by the United States and implemented by the Act.

The District Court heard evidence from both parties on the health risks of *hoasca* and the potential for diversion from the church. The Government presented evidence to the effect that use of *hoasca*, or DMT more generally, can cause psychotic reactions, cardiac irregularities, and adverse drug interactions. The UDV countered by citing studies documenting the safety of its sacramental use of *hoasca* and presenting evidence that minimized the likelihood of the health risks raised by the Government. With respect to diversion, the Government pointed to a general rise in the illicit use of hallucinogens, and cited interest in the illegal use of DMT and *hoasca* in particular; the UDV emphasized the thinness of any market for *hoasca*, the relatively small amounts of the substance imported by the church, and the absence of any diversion problem in the past.

The District Court concluded that the evidence on health risks was "in equipoise," [equally balanced] and similarly that the evidence on diversion was "virtually balanced." In the face of such an even showing, the court reasoned that the Government had failed to demonstrate a compelling interest justifying what it acknowledged was a substantial burden on the UDV's sincere religious exercise. The court also rejected the asserted interest in complying with the 1971 Convention on Psychotropic Substances, holding that the Convention does not apply to *hoasca*.

The court entered a preliminary injunction prohibiting the Government from enforcing the Controlled Substances Act with respect to the UDV's importation and use of *hoasca*. . . .

The Government does not challenge the District Court's factual findings or its conclusion that the evidence submitted on these issues was evenly balanced. Instead, the Government maintains that such evidentiary equipoise is an insufficient basis for issuing a preliminary injunction against enforcement of the Controlled Substances Act. . . .

The UDV effectively demonstrated that its sincere exercise of religion was substantially burdened, and the Government failed to demonstrate that the application of the burden to the UDV would, more likely than not, be justified by the asserted compelling interests. . . .

An Exception to Drug Laws Has Been Made for Native Americans

Under the . . . focused inquiry required by RFRA and the compelling interest test, the Government's mere invocation of the general characteristics of Schedule I substances, as set forth in the Controlled Substances Act, cannot carry the day. It is true, of course, that Schedule I substances such as DMT are exceptionally dangerous. Nevertheless, there is no indication that Congress, in classifying DMT, considered the harms posed by the particular use at issue here—the circumscribed, sacramental use of *hoasca* by the UDV. The question of the harms from the sacramental use of *hoasca* by the UDV *was* litigated below. Before the District Court found that the Government had not carried its burden of showing a compelling interest in preventing such harms, the court noted that it could not "ignore that the legislative branch of the government elected to place materials containing DMT on Schedule I of the [Act], reflecting findings that substances containing DMT have 'a high potential for abuse,' and 'no currently accepted medical use in treatment in the United States,' and that 'there is a lack of accepted safety for use of [DMT] under medical supervision.'" But Congress' determination that DMT should be listed under Schedule I simply does not provide a categorical answer that relieves the Government of the obligation to shoulder its burden under RFRA.

This conclusion is reinforced by the Controlled Substances Act itself. The Act contains a provision authorizing the Attorney General to "waive the requirement for registration of certain manufacturers, distributors, or dispensers if he finds it consistent with the public health and safety." The fact that the Act itself contemplates that exempting certain people from its requirements would be "consistent with the public health and safety" indicates that congressional findings with respect to Schedule I substances should not carry the determinative weight, for RFRA purposes, that the Government would ascribe to them.

And in fact an exception has been made to the Schedule I ban for religious use. For the past 35 years, there has been a regulatory exemption for use of peyote—a Schedule I substance—by the Native American Church. In 1994, Congress extended that exemption to all members of every recognized Indian Tribe. Everything the Government says about the DMT in *hoasca*—that, as a Schedule I substance, Congress has determined that it "has a high potential for abuse," "has no currently accepted medical use," and has "a lack of accepted safety for use . . . under medical supervision"—applies in equal measure to the mescaline in peyote, yet both the Executive and Congress itself have decreed an exception from the Controlled Substances Act for Native American religious use of peyote. If such use is permitted in the face of the congressional findings for hundreds of thousands of Native Americans practicing their faith, it is difficult to see how those same findings alone can preclude any consideration of a similar exception for the 130 or so American members of the UDV who want to practice theirs. . . .

The Government responds that there is a "unique relationship" between the United States and the Tribes, but never explains what about that "unique" relationship justifies overriding the same congressional findings on which the Government relies in resisting any exception for the UDV's religious use of *hoasca*. In other words, if any Schedule I substance is in fact *always* highly dangerous in any amount no matter how used, what about the unique relationship with the Tribes justifies allowing their use of peyote? Nothing about the unique political status of the Tribes makes their members immune from the health risks the Government asserts accompany any use of a Schedule I substance, nor insulates the Schedule I substance the Tribes use in religious exercise from the alleged risk of diversion.

The Government argues that the existence of a *congressional* exemption for peyote does not indicate that the Controlled Substances Act is amenable to *judicially crafted* exceptions. RFRA, however, plainly contemplates that *courts* would recognize exceptions—that is how the law works. . . .

Exceptions to Law Should Not Be Denied Without Cause

The well-established peyote exception also fatally undermines the Government's broader contention that the Controlled Substances Act establishes a closed regulatory system that admits of no exceptions under RFRA. The Government argues that the effectiveness of the Controlled Substances Act will be "necessarily . . . undercut" if the Act is not uniformly applied, without regard to burdens on religious exercise. Brief for Petitioners 18. The peyote exception, however, has been in place since the outset of the Controlled Substances Act, and there is no evidence that it has "undercut" the Government's ability to enforce the ban on peyote use by non-Indians.

The Government points to some pre-*Smith* cases relying on a need for uniformity in rejecting claims for religious exemptions under the Free Exercise Clause, but those cases strike us as quite different from the present one. Those cases did not embrace the notion that a general interest in uniformity justified a substantial burden on religious exercise; they instead scrutinized the asserted need and explained why the denied exemptions could not be accommodated. In *United States v.*

Lee, for example, the Court rejected a claimed exception to the obligation to pay Social Security taxes, noting that "mandatory participation is indispensable to the fiscal vitality of the social security system" and that the "tax system could not function if denominations were allowed to challenge the tax system because tax payments were spent in a manner that violates their religious belief." In *Braunfeld v. Brown*, the Court denied a claimed exception to Sunday closing laws, in part because allowing such exceptions "might well provide [the claimants] with an economic advantage over their competitors who must remain closed on that day." The whole point of a "uniform day of rest for all workers" would have been defeated by exceptions. These cases show that the Government can demonstrate a compelling interest in uniform application of a particular program by offering evidence that granting the requested religious accommodations would seriously compromise its ability to administer the program.

Here the Government's argument for uniformity is different; it rests not so much on the particular statutory program at issue as on slippery-slope concerns that could be invoked in response to any RFRA claim for an exception to a generally applicable law. The Government's argument echoes the classic rejoinder of bureaucrats throughout history: If I make an exception for you, I'll have to make one for everybody, so no exceptions. But RFRA operates by mandating consideration, under the compelling interest test, of exceptions to "rule[s] of general applicability." Congress determined that the legislated test "is a workable test for striking sensible balances between religious liberty and competing prior governmental interests." This determination finds support in our cases; in *Sherbert* for example, we rejected a slippery-slope argument similar to the one offered in this case, dismissing as "no more than a possibility" the State's speculation "that the filing of fraudulent claims by unscrupulous claimants feigning religious objections to Saturday work" would drain the unemployment benefits fund.

We reaffirmed just last Term the feasibility of case-by-case consideration of religious exemptions to generally applicable rules. In *Cutter v. Wilkinson* [see Chapter 3 of this book], we held that the Religious Land Use and Institutionalized Persons Act of 2000, which allows federal and state prisoners to seek religious accommodations pursuant to the same standard as set forth in RFRA, does not violate the Establishment Clause. We had "no cause to believe" that the compelling interest test "would not be applied in an appropriately balanced way" to specific claims for exemptions as they arose. Nothing in our opinion suggested that courts were not up to the task.

We do not doubt that there may be instances in which a need for uniformity precludes the recognition of exceptions to generally applicable laws under RFRA. But it would have been surprising to find that this was such a case, given the long-standing exemption from the Controlled Substances Act for religious use of peyote, and the fact that the very reason Congress enacted RFRA was to respond to a decision denying a claimed right to sacramental use of a controlled substance. And in fact the Government has not offered evidence demonstrating that granting the UDV an exemption would cause the kind of administrative harm recognized as a compelling interest in *Lee, Hernandez*, and *Braunfeld*. The Government failed to convince the District Court at the preliminary injunction hearing that health or diversion concerns provide a compelling interest in banning the UDV's sacramental use of *hoasca*. It cannot compensate for that failure now with the bold argument that there can be no RFRA exceptions at all to the Controlled Substances Act. . . .

The Government Failed to Demonstrate a Compelling Interest in Banning *Hoasca*

Before the District Court, the Government also asserted an interest in compliance with the 1971 United Nations Convention on Psychotropic Substances. The Convention, signed by the United States and implemented by the Controlled Substances Act, calls on signatories to prohibit the use of hallucinogens, including DMT. The Government argues that it has a compelling interest in meeting its international obligations by complying with the Convention.

The District Court rejected this interest because it found that the Convention does not cover *hoasca*. . .

We do not agree. . . . The fact that *hoasca* is covered by the Convention, however, does not automatically mean that the Government has demonstrated a compelling interest in applying the Controlled Substances Act, which implements the Convention, to the UDV's sacramental use of the tea. At the present stage, it suffices to observe that the Government did not even *submit* evidence addressing the international consequences of granting an exemption for the UDV. The Government simply submitted two affidavits by State Department officials attesting to the general importance of honoring international obligations and of maintaining the leadership position of the United States in the international war on drugs. We do not doubt the validity of these interests, any more than we doubt the general interest in promoting public health and safety by enforcing the Controlled Substances Act, but under RFRA invocation of such general interests, standing alone, is not enough.

The Government repeatedly invokes Congress' findings and purposes underlying the Controlled Substances Act, but Congress had a reason for enacting RFRA, too. Congress recognized that "laws 'neutral' toward religion may burden religious exercise as surely as laws intended to interfere with religious exercise," and legislated "the compelling interest test" as the means for the courts to "strik[e] sensible balances between religious liberty and competing prior governmental interests."

We have no cause to pretend that the task assigned by Congress to the courts under RFRA is an easy one. Indeed, the very sort of difficulties highlighted by the Government here were cited by this Court in deciding that the approach later mandated by Congress under RFRA was not required as a matter of constitutional law under the Free Exercise Clause. But Congress has determined that courts should strike sensible balances, pursuant to a compelling interest test that requires the Government to address the particular practice at issue. Applying that test, we conclude that the courts below did not err in determining that the Government failed to demonstrate, at the preliminary injunction stage, a compelling interest in barring the UDV's sacramental use of *hoasca.*

> *"The government's compelling interest in uniform enforcement should have been assessed in light of its obligation of evenhanded treatment for all similarly situated religious adherents."*

The Controlled Substances Act Should Be Enforced Without Exception, Even If This Limits Religious Freedom

Paul D. Clement, et al.

Paul D. Clement is the solicitor general of the United States. The following viewpoint is an excerpt from the brief he and other lawyers submitted to the U.S. Supreme Court, presenting the U.S. government's arguments for not allowing religious exceptions to the Controlled Substances Act (CSA). In it, they state the government's contention that the religious group Uniao do Vegetal should not be allowed to use the hallucinogenic drug hoasca*—also known as ayahuasca—in rituals because it is harmful and has a high potential for abuse. Further, they maintain that if the CSA is not enforced uniformly it will be impossible to control drug abuse and drug trafficking. If an exception is made for one church, it will have to be made for all others that want to use hallucinogens. The exception already made for Native American religions is not comparable, they say, because it applies only to members of federally recognized Indian tribes, who have a special relationship to the government.*

Paul D. Clement, et al., brief for the petitioners, *Gonzales, Attorney General, et al. v. O Centro Espirita Beneficiente Uniao do Vegetal et al.* U.S. Supreme Court, July, 2005.

The CSA [Controlled Substances Act] is one part of a larger legislative effort "to deal in a comprehensive fashion with the growing menace of drug abuse in the United States." Congress enacted the CSA as a "comprehensive" and "'closed' system of drug distribution" for all controlled substances, which strictly demarcates the drug transactions that are permitted, while rendering all "transactions outside the legitimate distribution chain illegal." Individual departures from that scheme are proscribed. Within that framework, Congress comprehensively banned the import, manufacture, distribution, possession, and use of Schedule I substances [dangerous drugs without medical uses] outside of tightly controlled research projects.

Congress itself placed DMT [dimethyltryptamine, a chemical ingredient of the drug *hoasca*] and any preparation containing DMT in Schedule I because they "ha[ve] a high potential for abuse," "ha[ve] no currently accepted medical use in treatment in the United States," and have "a lack of accepted safety for use . . . under medical supervision." That classification reflects a congressional judgment that DMT preparations warrant a categorical prohibition on importation, distribution, and use, rather than the regime of limited but highly regulated production and use provided for substances in the other Schedules.

Indeed, stanching the rapid expansion in the use of hallucinogens like DMT was of particular concern to Congress. At the time of the CSA's enactment, "hallucinogens accounted for the greatest single increase in drug offenses in the United States." Congress had before it evidence that DMT is a "known and abused" hallucinogen that has mind-altering effects "because of [its] direct action on the brain-cells." DMT's pharmacological properties are similar to LSD [lysergic acid]. DMT can precipitate psychoses, cause prolonged dissociative states, and can catalyze latent anxiety disorders. In fact, DMT was first listed as a dangerous controlled substance by the Food and Drug Administration in 1966 based on its "hallucinogenic effect" and "potential for abuse." . . .

The use of and trafficking in controlled substances "creates social harms of the first magnitude," *City of Indianapolis v. Edmond*, making drug abuse "one of the most serious problems confronting our society today." *National Treasury Employees Union v. Von Raab*. "Few problems affecting the health and welfare of our population, particularly our young, cause greater concern than the escalating use of controlled substances." *Harmelin v. Michigan*. Protecting the public from those threats to health and safety is a prototypical compelling governmental interest.

Congress's Findings Satisfy RFRA and Preclude Individual Religious Exemptions

The government has a compelling interest in the uniform enforcement of the CSA's Schedule I prohibitions. This Court repeatedly recognized in pre-*Smith* free exercise cases that certain vitally important statutory programs could not function consistent with a regime of religious exemptions. Those precedents include cases that unambiguously applied the same compelling interest test that RFRA [Religious Freedom Restoration Act] codifies. In each case, the comprehensiveness of the government's regulatory program, the legislature's narrow delineation of any viable exceptions, and the critical importance of the interests advanced by the programs combined to create a compelling interest in uniform enforcement that could not be advanced if subjected to piecemeal exemptions.

In light of the vital governmental interests in public health and safety served by the CSA, Congress's findings concerning the inherent dangerousness of Schedule I substances, the intractable law enforcement problems posed by drug trafficking, and the imperative of a comprehensive and closed regulatory scheme satisfy RFRA's compelling interest and least restrictive means inquiries.

First, Congress did not just find that DMT was "dangerous in the abstract." By placing it in Schedule I, Congress determined that DMT actually "has a high potential for abuse" and cannot be safely used even "under medical supervision." Congress further found that, for mind-altering hallucinogens like DMT, the potential for abuse extends to "*any* material, compound, mixture, or preparation which contains *any* quantity of" DMT (emphases added). The vital public health and safety interests served by the CSA thus are implicated by all uses under all conditions of all DMT-based substances, regardless of the user's motive or preference for delivery through a needle, pipe, or tea.

Congress's determination that a categorical ban is required encompasses the very individualized consideration and judgment that RFRA requires. Religious motivation does not change the science. The serious adverse "health effects caused by the use of controlled substances exist regardless of the motivation of the user," and as a result "the use of such substances, even for religious purposes, violates the very purpose of the laws that prohibit them."

Second, the CSA cannot function with its necessary rigor and comprehensiveness if subjected to judicial exemptions. Few law enforcement tasks have proved more formidable than the detection of unlawful drug usage and the prevention of drug abuse and diversion. Indeed, "the obstacles to detection of illegal conduct may be unmatched in any other area of law enforcement." . . .

Congress concluded that only a "closed system of drug distribution" would avert the significant dangers associated with the use of Schedule I drugs and combat the growing and intractable problems of drug abuse and drug trafficking. The effectiveness of that closed system will necessarily be undercut by judicially crafted exemptions on terms far more generous than the narrow clinical studies that Congress authorized.

With respect to Schedule I substances in particular, the very psychic and physiological features that render the drugs so dangerous also render them attractive to drug users and susceptible to abuse. . . .

The religious motives of the distributor or user do not change that drug culture or the law-enforcement realities. . . .

Exceptions Would Have to Be Made for Other Groups

Third, the court of appeals' foundational premise that religious exemptions could be cabined, so that the compelling interests served by the CSA would be unimpaired, blinks reality. The framework adopted by RFRA, pre-*Smith* precedent, and fundamental principles under the Religion Clauses, reinforced just last Term, see *Cutter* [Chapter 3 of this book], generally require that any religious exemption be extended to all similarly situated adherents. . . .

Indeed, the neutral accommodation command in RFRA, like the identically worded RLUIPA [Religious Land Use and Institutionalized Persons Act] standard, ensures that accommodations will be available in a non-discriminatory fashion.

For that reason, the government's compelling interest in uniform enforcement should have been assessed in light of its obligation of evenhanded treatment for all similarly situated religious adherents. At a minimum, an equivalent exemption will be demanded by other religious groups that use ayahuasca, like the Santo Daime Church and the "many [other] sects and individuals who use the tea." [Quoted from the Appendix to this brief.] While the Santo Daime Church has more broadly opened its hoasca ceremonies to others, courts may consider differences in evangelistic theology to be a tenuous basis for selectivity in governmental accommodations. Courts might also be concerned that a selective accommodation would effectively give the UDV [Uniao do Vegetal] a competitive advantage over the Santo Daime church in the religious "marketplace of ideas." Religious claimants seeking other hallucinogens (such as marijuana and LSD) will no doubt insist that they are similarly situated as well. . . .

Fourth, and relatedly, like the efforts to obtain medical or compassionate exemptions to Schedule I, claims for religious exemptions, once recognized, would proliferate. Under the court of appeals' decision, the CSA's hitherto closed and uniform enforcement scheme would give way to the independent, case-by-case judgments of more than 700 district court judges in countless cases based on dueling experts, personal testimonials, record differentials, journal articles, and judicial assessments of whether a particular drug or its delivery system qualifies as a "street drug" or as "esoteric." . . .

Indeed, an almost inevitable byproduct of court decisions under RFRA holding that Schedule I substances can be ingested safely enough in religious ceremonies is that the public will misread such rulings as indicating that a substance is not harmful, fueling an increase in its use. When fewer people believe a drug is harmful, illicit use of that drug expands. The need to prevent such misperceptions underscores the imperative of preserving the CSA's closed system for Schedule I drugs. . . .

In sum, the compelling public health and safety interests advanced by the CSA, the necessity of a comprehensive and closed statutory scheme to control drug distribution, the complex and intractable character of the drug abuse and drug trafficking problem, and the infeasibility of strictly cabining religious exemptions or coordinating drug enforcement with religious officials categorically establish that the government has a compelling interest in prohibiting religious uses of Schedule I substances which cannot be served by any less restrictive means. Using RFRA to bypass Congress's prescribed standards for assessing safety in this area of uniquely complex scientific judgments and unparalleled law enforcement problems would thwart Congress's compelling interests, not advance them by a less restrictive means.

Tribal Use of Peyote Is Distinct

Judge [Michael] McConnell [the court of appeals judge] erroneously viewed the federal exemption for peyote as evidencing Schedule I's amenability to an array of religious exemptions. In fact, the unique character of the peyote exemption proves the opposite. First, that exemption is fundamentally limited to and defined by the *sui generis* [unique] political status of Indian Tribes and the federal government's unique relationship with them. The statute permits ceremonial peyote use only by members of federally recognized Indian Tribes, which have a unique sovereign status within the United States. It does not permit the use of peyote—religious or otherwise—by non-Native Americans or by Native Americans who are not members of federally recognized Indian Tribes.

That unique inter-sovereign accommodation is a direct outgrowth of the United States' historic trust obligation towards Indian Tribes and duty to preserve tribal culture. . . . Moreover, exemptions for the ancient cultural practices of federally recognized Tribes are necessarily self-limiting and do not raise the same concerns about sectarian discrimination.

Second, Congress, not the courts, created the peyote exemption, . . . just one year after the passage of RFRA. If RFRA already authorized religious exemptions from Schedule I, then there was no need for Congress, in the wake of RFRA and fully cognizant of its existence, to enact the peyote exemption. . . .

RFRA does not require accommodations that imperil the health and safety of members of the public. Thus, even if RFRA requires some judicial examination of whether Congress's findings specifically preclude a requested religious exemption, the court of appeals fundamentally erred because, in making its predicate determinations about the safety and susceptibility to abuse and diversion of respondents' DMT preparation, the court failed to accord any significance, let alone substantial deference, to Congress's findings and judgment on those critical issues. . . .

Hoasca's Harmfulness

The district court acknowledged that the government provided a "great deal of evidence suggesting that hoasca may pose health risks to UDV members." DMT is a mind-altering hallucinogen with pharmacological properties similar to LSD. Respondents ingest hoasca at least 34 times a year, and administer the same tea to children and pregnant women.

Hoasca delivers DMT to the brain in an amount sufficient to produce a "significantly altered state of consciousness." More than half of the subjects in a hoasca study suffered cardiac [heart] irregularities. Hoasca also causes "alterations in the sensation of breathing or heartbeat, intestinal cramps, vomiting, diarrhea, an unsteady gait, or even [causes] fainting or falling down." [Quoted from the government case to the court of appeals.]

"Psychosis is definitely of most concern." Respondents' own experts acknowledged that hallucinogens as a class can precipitate psychoses and other adverse psychological reactions. The Medical-Scientific Department of the Brazilian UDV has acknowledged that hoasca poses "a possible risk of worsening a psychotic condition," and has documented numerous instances in which hoasca caused or contributed to psychotic episodes. UDV's leader, respondent Jeffrey Bronfman, describes ayahuasca as creating a "tremendous potential for fragmentation of the psyche" and producing "horrible and terrifying experiences." Respondents' expert too has recognized that hoasca ingestion can produce "nightmarish visionary experience[s]" and "turbulent states of consciousness." In addition, as respondents themselves acknowledge, hoasca poses a significant risk of dangerous adverse drug interactions, with what UDV Brazil describes as potentially "hazardous effects to the health."

Respondents submitted evidence that their particular religious setting "optimized safety and minimized the likelihood of adverse consequences." But, while a ceremonial setting may make DMT ingestion less dangerous than recreational use, it does not make it safe. The setting does not and cannot change the underlying biochemistry of the person or the pharmacology of the drug. . . .

Hoasca's Potential for Abuse and Diversion

Government experts explained that hoasca's hallucinogenic visions and euphoric effects create "a significant potential for abuse." First, DMT was a drug of abuse in the 1960s, and there has been a marked "resurgence in the abuse of hallucinogenic substances," with the illicit use of hallucinogens rising by 92% in the 1990s. Nearly 35 million persons have tried hallucinogens, including more than 10% of high school seniors. Respondents admit that there is "great interest" and "a *tremendous* amount of curiosity about 'ayahuasca' here in the United States." In addition, there is a "network of modern-day Shaman 'therapists'" in the United States who promote and use "psychedelic plant preparations," including ayahuasca, as respondents acknowledge. . . .

In addition, "hoasca use in Europe, often a helpful indicator for determining the possibility of the diversion in the United States, has risen *substantially* in recent years" (emphasis added) [petition to the court of appeals]. . . .

The Internet also documents expanding interest in the drug, with countless websites offering tourism packages to Brazil to participate in ayahuasca ceremonies, marketing and selling the substance or ingredients for making it, and extolling the hallucinogenic experiences provided by the tea. . . .

In rejecting Congress's judgment that this DMT preparation "has a high potential for abuse," the district court noted testimony about the alleged "thinness" of the market for DMT tea. But respondent Bronfman's own words prove otherwise: "Because of the great interest in 'ayahuasca' here," there are "financial rewards involved in having a supply to distribute." . . .

The district court also cited testimony that the volume imported would be relatively small. But that assumes that only UDV would be permitted to import and distribute hoasca, when in fact RFRA's protection would have to be extended to all similarly situated groups. Furthermore, the court presumed that the number of participants in UDV ceremonies would not expand and that UDV would engage in the bare minimum number of hoasca ceremonies, when in fact members of UDV Brazil "often" use hoasca "as frequently as several times per week. . . ."

Finally, both the district court and Judge McConnell suggested that the use of tea as a delivery system made it less likely to be diverted, because of its "bulky form," and its purportedly "esoteric" character which, Judge McConnell reasoned, distinguishes hoasca from "street drugs." But there is nothing "esoteric" about DMT, which has a long history of abuse in this country, and [according to the media] "is back in favor as a 'party drug,' used as a short-acting alternative to LSD." While DMT—which has been labeled "the businessman's trip"—may be abused as much on Wall Street as on more pedestrian streets, that distinction cannot reasonably justify judicial descheduling under RFRA. And, as the illegal smuggling of aliens and firearms attests, bulkiness is no hindrance to illicit trafficking. It certainly did not prevent UDV from bringing at least fourteen shipments of hoasca into the United States before the Customs Service discovered its true nature. Indeed, tea is a known delivery system for many controlled substances, from marijuana, to cocaine, to opium. No one would suggest that marijuana tea or coca tea is too "bulky" or "esoteric" to create diversion concerns that warrant the strictest regulation by Congress, and it makes no sense to conclude otherwise with respect to DMT.

"Once you read this case, you see really important doctrines that will protect religious freedom for decades."

There Is Now a Bright Future for Religious Liberty Cases

Kevin Eckstrom and Sarah Pulliam

Kevin Eckstrom is an associate editor at Religion News Service, which provides a daily news service covering all faiths to major publications. Sarah Pulliam is a news intern for Christianity Today. *In the following viewpoint they explain that the U.S. Supreme Court's ruling in favor of the right of a small sect to use hallucinogenic tea in religious rituals is significant both for the precedent it set and as evidence that the Court, under its new Chief Justice John Roberts, is likely to advocate religious liberty. Several major Christian legal groups had filed friend-of-the-court briefs because although they do not favor the use of drugs themselves, they saw this as a major test case with wide implications for the freedom of all groups to practice their faith without government interference.*

Some legal groups see Tuesday's Supreme Court "tea" decision as an important precedent in religious freedom jurisprudence. Others see it as a harbinger of church-state relations under the Roberts court. But religious freedom advocates agree that the case means it will likely be harder for the government to limit expression after the ruling.

The Court ruled unanimously in favor of a New Mexico sect's bid to use hallucinogenic tea in religious rituals. Seen as a major religious liberty test case, several Christian legal groups, including the National Association of Evangelicals, had filed friend-of-the-court briefs on behalf of the sect.

In his first religious freedom case, Chief Justice John Roberts said the sect's right to religious expression and practice superseded federal drug control laws that were used to confiscate the tea, known as hoasca.

Tuesday's ruling served as a strong endorsement of the 1993 Religious Freedom Restoration Act [RFRA], which requires the government to show a "compelling interest" before it can limit religious freedom. Roberts said the law gives courts the authority to "strike sensible balances" in weighing government regulation and religious expression.

Jared Leland, legal counsel for The Becket Fund for Religious Liberty in Washington, said the case is evidence that under Roberts, the Court will advocate religious liberty. "With a smile on my face, I can say that there is certainly a bright future for religious liberty cases," Leland said. "The case is greatly significant because of the fact that the teeth of the Religious Freedom Restoration Act were sharpened. It increased the level of protection for all faiths, especially less conventional faiths in the United States."

The Case Had Wide Implications

Religious groups had watched the case closely because it had wide implications for the right of all groups to practice their faith without risk of government interference. "Today it's something about hallucinogenic tea, but tomorrow it could be something that Roman Catholics or Southern Baptists or a number of groups need some accommodation in relation to a federal law," said Charles Haynes, senior scholar for the First Amendment Center.

Last year, the Supreme Court ruled that in the interest of the nation's drug war, an exception to the Controlled Substances Act could not be made to allow the production of marijuana for medical use.

The 130-member O Centro Espirita Beneficiente Uniao do Vegetal (UDV), said the tea that is brewed in the faith's Brazilian homeland gives members a "heightened spiritual awareness" that allows them to communicate with God. Members believe they can understand God only by drinking the tea, which is consumed twice a month at four-hour ceremonies.

The tea contains the drug dimethyltryptamine (DMT), which is banned under the 1970 Controlled Substances Act and a 1971 international treaty that bans its importation. Roberts rejected arguments that the use of hoasca threatened the drug law, and said the "circumscribed, sacramental use" of the drug for religious purposes could be allowed. "The government's argument echoes the classic rejoinder of bureaucrats throughout history: If I make an exception for you, I'll have to make one for everybody, so no exceptions," Roberts wrote. "But RFRA operates by mandating consideration, under the compelling interest test, of exceptions to 'rule[s] of general applicability.'"

Both Roberts and the UDV's lawyers noted that peyote—which also contains DMT—has been allowed for 35 years in Native American religious rites.

Kelly Shackelford, chief counsel for Liberty Legal Institute, said the institute argued in its friend-of-the-court brief that because the government already allows Native Americans to use peyote, the case was not compelling. "When they infringe on religious freedom, governments tend to theoretically argue that they have a compelling reason to interfere," Shackelford said. "This takes the mask off of those cases that say it's compelling."

Shackelford said the Court may not have found compelling interest in the case had it involved a larger religious group. "Are the facts of this case really important? No," he said. "But once you read this case, you see really important doctrines that will protect religious freedom for decades."

Roberts upheld two lower court decisions that said federal agents were wrong to confiscate the tea in 1999. The case now returns to lower courts, where the government is entitled to make its case more fully at a trial.

Justice Samuel Alito, the newest member of the Court, did not participate in arguments or the Court's decision, because the case was argued before he joined the bench.

"Our courts derive their legitimacy in part from their willingness to give reasoned explanations for their decisions. The hoasca opinion is well-reasoned as far as it goes, but it should have gone further."

The Court Failed to Address a Critical Ambiguity in Its Prior Rulings

Michael C. Dorf

Michael C. Dorf is a professor of law at Columbia University and is the author of two books. In the following viewpoint he explains how the U.S. Supreme Court's decision about a small sect's right to use the hallucinogenic tea hoasca *in religious rituals differed from prior rulings concerning free exercise of religion. He points out that it was inconsistent with the decision in an earlier case,* Employment Division v. Smith, *which involved the religious use of peyote, and yet it did not offer an explanation for the inconsistency. The precedent established in the* Smith *case was left intact, although the Court appears to have rejected the logic on which that precedent was based. In Dorf's opinion, its failure to clarify this ambiguity means that the same issues will probably return to the Court before long.*

Michael C. Dorf, "The Supreme Court's Unanimous Decision Recognizing a Religious Right to Use Hallucinogenic Tea," *FindLaw.com*, February 27, 2006. Reproduced by permission of the author and publisher.

Last week, in *Gonzales v. O Centro Espirita Beneficiente Uniao Do Vegetal*, the Supreme Court held that U.S. members of a Brazilian-based Christian Spiritist Sect had a right to use a hallucinogenic tea called hoasca for religious purposes. The Court so ruled notwithstanding the fact that hoasca is a Schedule I substance with no medical or otherwise accepted use.

Crucial to the reasoning of the unanimous opinion, authored by Chief Justice [John] Roberts, was the Court's determination that the government bore the burden of showing that permitting a religious exception to the prohibition would undermine compelling governmental objectives.

The Court's decision appears to indicate that the Justices are more receptive to claims of religious freedom now than they were just sixteen years ago, when they issued a landmark ruling in a case involving a different hallucinogenic drug—peyote—rejecting a claimed right to use the drug for religious purposes.

But it is not clear whether the Justices are really more receptive to such claims because the Court's hoasca opinion ignored, rather than addressed, a critical ambiguity in its own prior rulings.

The Nineteenth-Century Approach to Free Exercise Claims

To understand what makes the hoasca case important requires some familiarity with the Justices' less-than-entirely-successful efforts, over time, to reconcile the background assumption of majority rule with the First Amendment's protection of free exercise of religion.

The doctrinal story begins in the Nineteenth Century, at a time when the Mormon Church regarded polygamy as a religious rite. (The Mormon Church prohibited the practice in 1890.) George Reynolds was charged with violating a federal law banning bigamy. He defended on the ground that he was obligated to take plural wives by his religion. But the trial judge refused to instruct the jury that sincere religious belief could excuse compliance with an otherwise valid law. Reynolds was convicted.

The Supreme Court affirmed the conviction in the 1878 case of *Reynolds v. United States.* Chief Justice [Morrison R.] Waite explained: "Laws are made for the government of actions, and while they cannot interfere with mere religious belief and opinions, they may with practices." A religious belief in the necessity of human sacrifice could not supply a defense to murder, the Court reasoned, and more generally, to grant exemptions from generally applicable laws on the basis of individual religious belief would be "to permit every citizen to become a law unto himself."

There the law stood for nearly a century, but then the Supreme Court ruled that sincere religious belief can excuse compliance with otherwise valid general laws, unless the government can demonstrate that it has a "compelling interest" that cannot be achieved by granting religious exemptions. Under this test, human sacrifice would still be proscribable because of the government's compelling interest in protecting innocent human life, but less pressing governmental objectives would yield to religious claims.

Two leading cases illustrate what the compelling interest test requires. In 1963, in *Sherbert v. Verner*, the Court invalidated a South Carolina law that deemed a Seventh Day Adventist ineligible for unemployment benefits because she refused to work on Saturdays. Even though the law applied to everyone, the Court held, as applied to those who observed the Sabbath on Saturday, it infringed religious freedom.

Likewise, in the 1972 ruling in *Wisconsin v. Yoder* [see Chapter 1 of this book] the Supreme Court found that Wisconsin had failed to justify the application of its compulsory education law with respect to Amish children between the ages of 14 and 15. (The state required children to go to school until the age of 16; for religious reasons, the Amish finished school after the eighth grade.)

The Peyote Decision, and the Reaction of Congress

In 1990, however, in the case of *Employment Division v. Smith*, the Court essentially returned to the principle of *Reynolds*. Echoing the *Reynolds* Court's unwillingness to make every citizen "a law unto himself," Justice [Antonin] Scalia, writing for the majority in *Smith*, declared that "a private right to ignore generally applicable laws . . . is a constitutional anomaly."

Accordingly, in the *Smith* case itself, the Justices did not apply the compelling interest test to Oregon's extension of its ban of peyote to those who used this hallucinogenic drug in their Native American worship service. Thus, the majority ruled that the Oregon law did not even implicate the religious rights of Native Americans.

Since the *Smith* decision in 1990, the Court has understood the Free Exercise Clause to be nothing more than a principle of formal equality: If a law singles out a religious practice because it is religious, then the compelling interest test applies. But if the law applies to everyone, then no Free Exercise issue is even raised.

For example, under *Smith*, a state could not specifically prohibit the wearing of yarmulkes in courtrooms, for that would single out observant Jews for disadvantage. But the state could forbid the wearing of all headgear in courtrooms, even though the impact on observant Jews of these two laws is identical.

The *Smith* ruling was widely unpopular, sparking legislation in 1993 that enjoyed broad bipartisan support: the federal Religious Freedom Restoration Act (RFRA). That law expressly restored the compelling interest test even for generally applicable laws, wherever they substantially burden religious exercises.

The Court Strikes Back by Invalidating RFRA

Yet Congress did not have the last word. In the 1997 case of *City of Boerne v. Flores*, the Supreme Court held that RFRA itself was unconstitutional. Congress may only exercise those powers delegated to it by the Constitution. Although Congress claimed that RFRA was authorized by Section Five of the Fourteenth Amendment, the Court thought otherwise.

Section Five grants to Congress the power to "enforce" the substantive provisions of the Fourteenth Amendment, including its Due Process Clause. That Due Process Clause is the basis for the application of the First Amendment's Free Exercise Clause to state and local governments. Hence, Congress thought that, by "restoring" the compelling interest test and the pre-*Smith* cases, it was "enforcing" the Fourteenth Amendment—and thus acting within its constitutionally granted powers.

The Court disagreed. In *Boerne*, Justice [Anthony] Kennedy explained for the Court that the power to enforce the substantive provisions of the Fourteenth Amendment does not include the power to change the meaning of those substantive provisions. The Court had already said—in *Smith*—that the compelling interest test does not apply to laws that do not single out religious practices. Accordingly, RFRA's attempt to restore the rule of *Sherbert* and *Yoder* was deemed a disguised effort to change the meaning of Free Exercise and Due Process. And the only way to do that is by amending the Constitution.

The Exaggerated Rumors of RFRA's Demise

The *Boerne* case thus held RFRA unconstitutional, but it left a critical ambiguity unaddressed. By its terms, RFRA applied to all levels of government—federal, state and local. The *Boerne* decision itself involved a local law, and its theory made clear that Congress was without power to subject local or state laws of general applicability to the compelling interest test. But what about federal laws?

As to federal laws, most constitutional scholars (including yours truly) argued that RFRA remained valid. Why? Because as to federal laws, Congress did not need to rely on its power to enforce the Fourteenth Amendment for authority to enact RFRA. Rather, with respect to federal laws, RFRA was simply an exception to whatever other rules Congress enacted—for example, the drug laws. It said, in effect, don't apply these other federal laws to the extent that they substantially burden free exercise of religion and fail the compelling interest test.

Congress surely didn't need any source of power to withhold the exercise of federal authority. Put differently, the authority for RFRA as applied to the federal government was simply whatever power authorized each of the laws to which RFRA mandated an exception.

In last week's ruling in the hoasca case, the Supreme Court tacitly accepted this theory. It remarked in a footnote that the Court had invalidated RFRA as to state and local government in *Boerne*, and it proceeded on the assumption that, with respect to the federal drug laws, RFRA could simply be treated as authorization for the courts to find religious exemptions from those laws.

It is not very surprising that the Court upheld RFRA as applied to the federal government. What is somewhat surprising is that it did so unanimously, and without even addressing two arguments that had previously been advanced in support of the proposition that RFRA is unconstitutional as applied to all levels of government.

Establishment of Religion: The First Dog That Didn't Bark

According to the first argument, which was made by Justice [John Paul] Stevens in a concurring opinion in the *Boerne* case, RFRA was unconstitutional because it favored religious claims for exemptions from general laws over other kinds of exemptions, in violation of the First Amendment's Establishment Clause.

The Court has long held that government may not favor religion over non-religion. Yet RFRA can be seen as doing just that. If you can't work on Saturdays because that is your Sabbath, then RFRA—which expressly approves of the *Sherbert* decision—will grant you an exemption from a state law that classifies you as ineligible for unemployment compensation. However, if you can't work on Saturdays because that is the only day that you can feasibly visit your ailing mother, RFRA provides you no excuse (unless perhaps you can claim that you need to visit your mother to comply with the Biblical obligation to honor her). More generally, RFRA favors those who claim religious reasons for exemptions from general laws over those who claim medical, family and other non-religious reasons for exemptions.

Look at last week's decision itself. The Court held that the federal government bore the burden of proving that granting a religious exemption from the general prohibition on hoasca possession would undermine the prohibition. Yet less than a year ago, in *Gonzales v. Raich*, the Court had placed the burden of showing that an exemption from a general prohibition on marijuana use would not undermine the prohibition on the law's challengers—not on the government defending the law.

The difference in burden allocation mattered: The federal government was permitted to enforce its marijuana prohibition nothwithstanding a medical claim rooted in states' rights; it was not permitted to enforce its hoasca prohibition in the face of a religious claim.

Does Justice Stevens's argument mean that the Court was wrong in the hoasca case? Should the Justices have invalidated RFRA as applied to all levels of government?

Not necessarily. Recall that only Justice Stevens had previously expressed the view that RFRA violates the Establishment Clause. Other Justices might have reasonably thought that a regime of religious exemptions does not actually favor religion over non-religion. Rather, such a regime provides protection for religious minorities who might fare poorly in the political process. After all, it is no accident that during the era of Prohibition, ritual use of wine (by Catholics, Jews and others) was permitted, but that Oregon and other states made no exception for ritual use of peyote. RFRA, on this view, merely levels the playing field.

And indeed, that is more or less what the Supreme Court said last year in *Cutter v. Wilkinson* [see Chapter 3 of this book]. That case rejected an Establishment Clause challenge to a different law—the Religious Land Use and Institutionalized Persons Act (RLUIPA)—which, like RFRA, mandates that general laws (in the context of prisons and other settings of confinement) be subject to the compelling interest test if they substantially burden religious practice. (Curiously, Justice Stevens joined the majority opinion in *Cutter* without explaining whether, or why, he had changed his mind since writing his concurring opinion in *Boerne*.)

Separation of Powers: The Second Dog That Didn't Bark

A second argument for the invalidity of RFRA even as applied to the federal government derives from the language of the peyote decision itself. Legislatures, Justice Scalia wrote there, could balance the costs and benefits of granting religious exemptions in particular cases, but courts are particularly ill-suited to that task: Weighing the importance of a religious practice against the government interest in its generally applicable laws is within the legislature's competence, not that of the courts.

Yet if the judiciary lacks the institutional competence to perform some task, how can the legislature assign that task to the judiciary? In the view suggested by this rhetorical question, RFRA violated the separation of powers—the constitutional notion that each branch of government must stick to its assigned area of expertise.

In his opinion for the Court in the hoasca case, Chief Justice Roberts addressed the separation-of-powers objection obliquely. He said that concerns about judicial competence led the *Smith* Court to reject the compelling interest test as a matter of constitutional obligation. But, he implied, those concerns are not weighty enough to override a Congressional mandate—in RFRA—to apply the compelling interest test.

The Court Fails to Address Judicial Competence Concerns

Why not? Is it because judicial application of the compelling interest test is merely difficult—rather than, as suggested in the peyote case, impossible? And if so, does that suggest that the peyote case itself was wrongly decided? Why should the Court shy away from performing its constitutional duty merely because doing so is difficult? Persuasive answers could perhaps be given to these questions, but the Court did not even address them.

To be fair to the Court, perhaps Chief Justice Roberts ignored the separation-of-powers argument in the hoasca case because it was not advanced by the parties. Avoiding unnecessary determinations of constitutional law is an important discipline for the Court.

At the same time, however, the Court has an obligation to explain apparent inconsistencies in its own decisions. Moreover, if, as the *Smith* Court suggested, it is simply improper for the judiciary to apply the compelling interest test in religion cases, then the fact that the parties didn't object to the courts' playing this improper role should not have made any difference.

Our courts derive their legitimacy in part from their willingness to give reasoned explanations for their decisions. The hoasca opinion is well-reasoned as far as it goes, but it should have gone further in explaining just what, if anything, is left of the Court's broad pronouncements in the peyote case. There, Justice Scalia wrote for the Court that it is an "unavoidable consequence of democratic government" that the legislature must make religious exemption determinations on a statute-by-statute basis rather than having the courts weigh each law against claims to religious freedom under the compelling interest test. The disadvantage that thus results to religious minorities, the *Smith* majority said, "must be preferred to a system in which each conscience is a law unto itself or in which judges weigh the social importance of all laws against the centrality of all religious beliefs."

In the hoasca case, the Court formally left *Smith* intact as the constitutional rule. Yet, at the same time, the Court appeared to reject the core logic of *Smith*, as Justice Scalia explicated it. Thus, these issues will likely return to the Court before too long.

"This reaffirmation that the 'least restrictive means' and 'compelling interest' requirements are not toothless is one that should shape courts' interpretations and applications of many other *religious-accommodations laws."*

Separation of Church and State Is a Means of Implementing Religious Freedom

Richard Garnett

Richard Garnett is an associate professor at the University of Notre Dame's law school. In the following viewpoint he states that the U.S. Supreme Court's opinion on the right of O Centro Espirita Beneficiente Uniao do Vegetal (UDV) to use hallucinogenic tea in religious ceremonies may tell more about the current and future state of constitutional law than more highly publicized cases. It is especially significant, he says, that the opinion was unanimous, which shows that although the judges are sharply divided on some church-state issues, they are united in recognizing that the Constitution permits—but does not require—special accommodations of religion. The separation of church and state is not an antireligious ideology, as some people assume; rather, it is a means of implementing the principle of religious freedom.

Richard Garnett, "An Unassuming Decision," *National Review Online*, February 23, 2006. Reproduced by permission.

With all the news, commentary, and frantic spin attending the Supreme Court's decision to review the federal ban on partial-birth abortion, it would be easy to overlook the justices' recent opinion in a religious-freedom case involving the sacramental use of hallucinogenic tea from the Amazon. Certainly the (unsurprising) announcement about the abortion law is a headline-grabber, and sets the stage for a battle royal in the courts of both law and public opinion. That said, the sacramental-tea decision in *Gonzales v. O Centro Espirita Beneficiente Uniao do Vegetal* might tell us more about the current state and the future of constitutional law and, more generally, about the new Roberts Court.

In his crisp and straightforward opinion—from which no justice dissented—Chief Justice [John] Roberts reported that O Centro Espirita Beneficiente Uniao do Vegetal (UDV) is "a Christian Spiritist sect based in Brazil, with an American branch of approximately 130 individuals." And, he continued, "central to the UDV's faith is receiving communion through *hoasca* . . . , a sacramental tea made from two plants unique to the Amazon region." However, this tea includes a hallucinogenic substance that is strictly regulated by federal drug laws. After customs inspectors seized a shipment to the UDV of *hoasca*, the group filed a lawsuit, seeking an exemption from those laws and claiming that the application to them of the *hoasca* ban substantially burdens its free exercise of religion.

The Supreme Court decided 15 years ago, in *Employment Div. v. Smith*, that the Constitution itself does not *require* the government to accommodate religious believers by exempting their rituals, liturgies, and practices from the reach of generally applicable laws. That is, if the law says no speeding, the First Amendment does not require an exception for faith-based drag-racing; if hunting bald eagles is prohibited, there is no constitutional right to kill them and use their feathers in religious ceremonies. Of course, the free-exercise clause does not permit governments to single out religious believers and activities for discrimination or special burdens. Nor does it permit the state to punish people because of their religious beliefs. But when it comes to securing special exemptions from general laws, the Court has told believers to look to the political process—to make their case in the public square—and not to the Constitution.

The Religious Freedom Restoration Act

And so the UDV invoked the Religious Freedom Restoration Act [RFRA], a law passed by Congress in 1993 precisely in order to provide more generous accommodations of religion than the First Amendment requires. Under the act, the federal government may not "substantially burden" a person's exercise of religion, even through the imposition of generally applicable laws, unless it is the "least restrictive means" of advancing a "compelling" public interest.

The UDV won in the trial court, where the judge concluded that the government had failed to satisfy the act's standard, and to justify its insistence on a no-exceptions *hoasca* ban. The federal court of appeals affirmed the decision. Next, in the Supreme Court, the government argued, among other things, that the federal drug laws establish a "closed system." It conceded that the laws burden the UDV's religious exercise, but nevertheless asserted that the simple fact that the Controlled Substances Act designates the hallucinogenic substance in *hoasca* as unsafe and highly susceptible to abuse should preclude any consideration, even under the religious-freedom law, of individualized exceptions for religious users.

In their February 21 opinion, Chief Justice Roberts and his colleagues rejected resoundingly this argument, insisting that the government cannot justify substantial burdens on religious exercise by asserting that uniformity is required. The chief justice emphasized that the religious-accommodations law "contemplate[s] an inquiry more focused than the Government's categorical approach. RFRA requires the Government to demonstrate that the compelling interest test is satisfied through application of the challenged law to . . . the particular claimant whose sincere exercise of religion is being substantially burdened." This is exactly right. As church-state expert Professor Thomas Berg put it, this is how RFRA "ensures that there will be a balance between religious freedom and government interests: if the government could define its interest as uniform enforcement of the law, it would always win." In any event, as the Court pointed out, the government has for years allowed religious use of another illegal drug—peyote. Given this longstanding accommodation, it is all the more difficult to credit the government's claim that its preference for exceptionless uniformity in the application of the drug laws should automatically outweigh religious-freedom interests.

Two Points Worth Highlighting

There is more that could be said about this case and its significance. For now, though, two points are worth highlighting: *First*, like the Court's decision last year in *Cutter v. Wilkinson* [see Chapter 3 of this book]—which rejected the argument that another religious-accommodations law, the Religious Land Use and Institutionalized Persons Act, was an illegal "establishment" of religion—the ruling in *O Centro Espirita* was unanimous. True, the justices have been and remain sharply divided in church-state cases involving public displays and government funds; but when it comes to legislative accommodations of religious exercise, they are united in recognizing that the Constitution—*permits* special accommodations of religion and in insisting that accommodations laws secured through the political process should be meaningfully enforced. The fact that the Constitution rarely requires accommodations and exemptions does not and should not mean that they are or should be disfavored. And, *second*: This reaffirmation that the "least restrictive means" and "compelling interest" requirements are not toothless is one that should shape courts' interpretations and applications of many *other* religious-accommodations laws, federal and state.

Thinkers from St. Augustine and Pope Gregory VII to [seventeenth-century British theologian] Roger Williams and [U.S. president] James Madison have taught us that the "separation of church and state," properly understood, is an important component of religious freedom. That is, the *institutional and jurisdictional separation* of religious and political authority, the independence of religion from government oversight and control, respect for the freedom of individual conscience, government neutrality with respect to different religious traditions, and a strict rule against formal religious tests for public office—all these "separationist" features of our constitutional order have helped religious faith to thrive in America. Properly understood, the separation of church and state is not an anti-religious ideology, but rather, as [Catholic theologian] John Courtney Murray put it, a "means, a technique, [and] a policy to implement the principle of religious freedom." And, as the Court's decision reminds us, one permissible and praiseworthy way to implement this principle is through popularly enacted, reasonable, and balanced religious-accommodations laws.

Organizations to Contact

The editors have compiled the following list of organizations concerned with the issues debated in this book. The descriptions are derived from materials provided by the organizations. All have publications or information available for interested readers. The list was compiled on the date of publication of the present volume; the information provided here may change. Be aware that many organizations take several weeks or longer to respond to inquiries, so allow as much time as possible.

American Center for Law and Justice (ACLJ)
P.O. Box 90555, Washington, DC 20090
Web site: www.aclj.org

The ACLJ, which is operated by the nonprofit religious organization Christian Advocates Serving Evangelism, specializes in constitutional law and is dedicated to the idea that religious freedom and freedom of speech are inalienable, God-given rights. The center's purpose is to educate, promulgate, conciliate, and where necessary, litigate, to ensure that those rights are protected under the law. It offers phone and fax legal helplines. Audio and video files of its radio and television broadcasts are available at its Web site.

American Civil Liberties Union (ACLU)
125 Broad St., 18th Floor, New York, NY 10004
Web site: www.aclu.org

The ACLU is a large national organization that works to preserve First Amendment rights—freedom of speech, freedom of association and assembly, freedom of the press, and freedom of religion supported by the strict separation of church and state—as well as the right to equal protection under the law regardless of race, sex, religion, or national origin; the right to due process; and the right to freedom from unwarranted government intrusion into personal and private affairs.

It provides legal assistance in cases that involve these rights. Its Web site offers many articles and it can be contacted for more information through online forms.

Americans for Religious Liberty
P.O. Box 6656, Silver Spring, MD 20916
(301) 260-2988 • fax: (301) 260-2989
e-mail: info@arlinc.org
Web site: www.arlinc.org

The mission of Americans for Religious Liberty is to defend the core constitutional principle of separation of church and state. In its quarter century of activism in defense of church-state separation and freedom of conscience, it has been involved in over sixty actions in the courts. Its Web site offers a few articles, plus many print publications that can be purchased by mail.

Americans United for Separation of Church and State
518 C St., NE, Washington, DC 20002
(202) 466-3234 • fax: (202) 466-2587
e-mail: americansunited@au.org
Web site: www.au.org

Americans United (AU) is an independent nonprofit organization that protects separation of church and state by working on a wide range of pressing political and social issues. As a nonsectarian, nonpartisan organization, AU's membership includes Christians, Jews, Buddhists, people with no religious affiliation, and others. It publishes the monthly magazine *Church & State*, containing many detailed articles about court cases and other news concerning religious liberty, of which archives are available at its Web site.

Baptist Joint Committee for Religious Liberty
200 Maryland Ave. NE, Washington, DC 20002
(202) 544-4226 • fax: (202) 544-2094
e-mail: bjc@bjconline.org
Web site: www.bjconline.org

The mission of the Baptist Joint Committee for Religious Liberty is to defend and extend God-given religious liberty for all, furthering the Baptist heritage that champions the principle that religion must be freely exercised, neither advanced nor inhibited by government. Its Web site contains many articles dealing with religious liberty and the separation of church and state.

Becket Fund for Religious Liberty
1350 Connecticut Ave. NW, Suite 605
Washington, DC 20036
(202) 955-0095 • fax: (202) 955-0090
Web site: www.becketfund.org

The Becket Fund for Religious Liberty is a nonprofit, nonpartisan, interfaith, legal, and educational institute dedicated to protecting the free expression of all religious traditions. It believes that religious people and institutions are entitled to participate in government affairs on an equal basis with everyone else, and should not be excluded for professing their faith. It publishes a newsletter and its Web site contains information about litigation in which it is involved.

First Amendment Center
1207 18th Ave. S., Nashville, TN 37212
(615) 727-1600 • fax: (615) 727-1319
e-mail: info@fac.org
Web site: www.firstamendmentcenter.org

The First Amendment Center, which is affiliated with Vanderbilt University, works to preserve and protect First Amendment freedoms through information and education. The center serves as a forum for the study and exploration of free-expression issues, including freedom of speech, of the press and of religion, and the rights to assemble and to petition the government. Its Web site offers many articles and reports related to religious liberty.

Institute on Religion and Public Policy
1620 I St NW, Suite LL10, Washington, DC 20006
(202) 835-8760 • fax (202) 835-8764
e-mail: irpp@religionandpolicy.org
Web site: www.religionandpolicy.org

The Institute on Religion and Public Policy is an international, interreligious, nonprofit organization dedicated to ensuring freedom of religion as the foundation for security, stability, and democracy. It works globally with government policy makers, religious leaders, nongovernmental organizations, and others in order to develop, protect, and promote fundamental rights—especially the right of religious freedom. Its Web site contains information about programs in which it is involved.

International Religious Liberty Association (IRLA)
12501 Old Columbia Pike, Silver Spring, MD 20904
(301) 680-6686 • fax (301) 680-6695
e-mail: info@irla.org
Web site: www.irla.org

IRLA is a nonprofit, nonpartisan educational organization. Its mission is to disseminate the principles of religious liberty throughout the world; to defend and safeguard the civil right of all people to worship, to adopt a religion or belief of their choice, and to manifest their religious convictions in observance, promulgation, and teaching, subject only to the respect for the equivalent rights of others; and to support the right of religious organizations to operate freely in every country. It publishes a journal, *Fides et Libertas*; archives are available at its Web site, along with many other documents.

North American Religious Liberty Association (NARLA)
12501 Old Columbia Pike, Silver Spring, MD 20904
(301) 680-6683 • fax (301) 680-6695
e-mail: narla@religiousliberty.info
Web site: http://religiousliberty.info

NARLA, which is affiliated with the Seventh-day Adventist Church, exists to ensure that all peaceful people of faith are accorded the fundamental right not only to hold their beliefs but to actively practice their faith. It also works to ensure that religion is not co-opted by the state through direct regulation or through financial control. It publishes the monthly magazine *Liberty*, containing articles about religious freedom; archives are available at www.libertymagazine.org.

People for the American Way
2000 M Street NW, Suite 400, Washington, DC 20036
(202) 467-4999
e-mail: pfaw@pfaw.org
Web site: www.pfaw.org

People for the American Way is a nonprofit educational organization that is engaged in lobbying and other forms of political activism. Its purpose is to affirm "the American Way," by which it means pluralism; individuality; freedom of thought, expression, and religion; a sense of community; and tolerance and compassion for others. It is strongly opposed to the views of the "Religious Right" and to introduction of prayer or religious teachings in public schools. Its Web site contains press releases about recent and upcoming court cases that involve religious freedom.

Pew Forum on Religion & Public Life
1615 L Street NW, Suite 700, Washington, DC 20036
(202) 419-4550 • fax: (202) 419-4559
Web site: http://pewforum.org

The Pew Forum on Religion & Public Life is a nonpartisan, nonadvocacy organization that seeks to promote a deeper understanding of issues at the intersection of religion and public affairs. It pursues its mission by delivering timely, impartial information to national opinion leaders, including government officials and journalists, but does not take positions on policy debates. At its Web site there are many surveys and event transcripts as well as publications, and it also offers both an e-mail newsletter and an RSS news feed.

Religious Freedom Coalition
P.O. Box 77511, Washington, DC 20013
(202) 543-0300
e-mail: support@rfcnet.org
Web site: www.rfcnet.org

The Religious Freedom Coalition is a nonprofit educational organization dedicated to the equality of all humankind and the freedom of religious expression. It promotes religious freedom and family-based legislation. It publishes an e-mail newsletter, with archives available at its Web site.

Supreme Court of the United States Public Information Officer, Supreme Court of the United States
Washington, DC 20543
Web site: www.supremecourtus.gov

The Supreme Court's official Web site contains detailed descriptions of the Court and how it operates. It also has briefs, transcripts of oral arguments, and opinions in recent cases, as well as information about scheduled cases.

U.S. Department of Justice, First Freedom Project, Special Counsel for Religious Discrimination, Office of the Assistant Attorney General, Civil Rights Division
950 Pennsylvania Ave. NW,Washington, DC 20530
(202) 353-8622
e-mail: FirstFreedom@usdoj.gov
Web site: www.usdoj.gov/crt/religdisc

This government project was established in February 2007 to ensure commitment to continued expansion of enforcement of civil rights statutes protecting religious liberty. It will initiate regional seminars around the country to educate religious, civil rights, and community leaders, attorneys, government officials, and other interested citizens about the laws protecting religious freedom enforced by the Department of Justice and how to file complaints. Its Web site contains a detailed report on enforcement of laws protecting religious freedom, information about those laws, various pamphets in PDF format, and the bimonthly newsletter *Freedom in Focus.*

For Further Research

Books

Henry Julian Abraham and Barbara A. Perry, *Freedom and the Court: Civil Rights and Liberties in the United States*. 8th ed. Lawrence: University Press of Kansas, 2003.

John Anderson, *Religious Liberty in Transitional Societies: The Politics of Religion*. New York: Cambridge University Press, 2003.

Kathryn Page Camp, *In God We Trust: How the Supreme Court's First Amendment Decisions Affect Organized Religion*. Grand Haven, MI: FaithWalk Publishing, 2006.

Catharine Cookson, *Regulating Religion: The Courts and the Free Exercise Clause*. New York: Oxford University Press, 2001.

Derek H. Davis and Barry Hankins, eds., *New Religious Movements and Religious Liberty in America*. 2nd ed. Waco, TX: Baylor University Press, 2003.

Bruce J. Dierenfield, *The Battle over School Prayer: How* Engel v. Vitale *Changed America*. Lawrence: University Press of Kansas, 2007.

Michael C. Dorf, ed, *Constitutional Law Stories*. New York: Foundation, 2004.

Christopher L. Eisgruber and Lawrence G. Sager, *Religious Freedom and the Constitution*. Cambridge, MA: Harvard University Press, 2007.

Garrett Epps, *To an Unknown God: Religious Freedom on Trial*. New York: St. Martin's, 2001.

Noah Feldman, *Divided by God: America's Church-State Problem—and What We Should Do About It*. New York: Farrar, Straus and Giroux, 2005.

Louis Fisher, *Religious Liberty in America: Political Safeguards*. Lawrence: University Press of Kansas, 2002.

Ronald B. Flowers, *That Godless Court? Supreme Court Decisions on Church-State Relationships*. 2nd ed. Louisville, KY: Westminter John Knox, 2005.

Patrick M. Garry, *Wrestling with God: The Courts' Tortuous Treatment of Religion*. Washington, DC: Catholic University of America Press, 2006.

Kent Greenawalt, *Does God Belong in Public Schools?* Princeton, NJ: Princeton University Press, 2005.

———, *Religion and the Constitution: Volume I: Free Exercise and Fairness*. Princeton, NJ: Princeton University Press, 2006.

Marci A. Hamilton, *God vs. the Gavel: Religion and the Rule of Law*. New York: Cambridge University Press, 2005.

Phillip E. Hammond, David W. Machacek, and Eric Michael Mazur, *Religion on Trial: How Supreme Court Trends Threaten Freedom of Conscience in America*. Walnut Creek, CA: AltaMira, 2004.

Bryan Hilliard, *The U.S. Supreme Court and Medical Ethics*. St. Paul, MN: Paragon House, 2004.

Carolyn N. Long, *Religious Freedom and Indian Rights: The Case of* Oregon v. Smith. Lawrence: University Press of Kansas, 2000.

William Lee Miller, *The First Liberty: America's Foundation in Religious Freedom*. Washington, DC: Georgetown University Press, 2003.

David M. O'Brien, *Animal Sacrifice and Religious Freedom*: Church of the Lukumi Babalu Aye v. City of Hialeah. Lawrence: University Press of Kansas, 2004.

Shawn Francis Peters, *The Yoder Case: Religious Freedom, Education, and Parental Rights*. Lawrence: University Press of Kansas, 2003.

Huston Smith, *A Seat at the Table: Huston Smith in Conversation with Native Americans on Religious Freedom*. Berkeley: University of California Press, 2006.

Steven D. Smith, *Getting over Equality: A Critical Diagnosis of Religious Freedom in America*. New York: New York University Press, 2001.

Winnifred Fallers Sullivan, *The Impossibility of Religious Freedom*. Princeton, NJ: Princeton University Press, 2005.

Periodicals

Nate Anderson, "Liberty and Justice for the Small," *Christianity Today*, December 2006.

J. Kenneth Blackwell, "Religious Liberty," *Vital Speeches of the Day*, October 15, 2003.

Rob Boston, "Nine Justices, Ten Commandments, 2 Important Cases," *Church & State*, April 2005.

———, "The Religious Right and American Freedom," *Church & State*, June 2006.

Angelo M. Codevilla, "The Atheist Foxhole," *American Spectator*, February 2006.

Derek H. Davis, "A Commentary on the Supreme Court's 'Equal Treatment' Doctrine as the New Constitutional Paradigm for Protecting Religious Liberty," *Journal of Church & State*, Autumn 2004.

———, "Reacting to France's Ban: Headscarves and Other Religious Attire in American Public Schools," *Journal of Church & State*, Spring 2004.

Edd Doerr, "Gathering Storms," *Humanist*, November/December 2004.

Susanna Dokupil, "Defending History," *American Enterprise*, June 2005.

Benjamin Dowling-Sendor, "The Ten Commandments Rulings," *American School Board Journal*, October 2005.

———, "A Wise Neutrality," *American School Board Journal*, April 2004.

Robert F. Drinan, "The Court & Religion," *Commonweal*, November 21, 2003.

———, "A Victory for Religious Freedom," *National Catholic Reporter*, March 31, 2006.

Richard W. Garnett, "How High a Wall?" *Commonweal*, May 20, 2005.

Robert P. George and Gerard V. Bradley, "Barring Faith," *Weekly Standard*, July 17, 2006.

Joshua Green, "Roy and His Rock," *Atlantic*, October 2005.

Brad A. Greenberg, "Hide Your Bible," *Christianity Today*, July 2006.

Linda Greenhouse, "Justices Allow a Commandments Display, Bar Others," *New York Times*, June 28, 2005.

Marci A. Hamilton, "Room for Religion," *Christian Century*, August 9, 2005.

James F. Harris, "Religion and Liberal Democracy," *Humanist*, May/June 2006.

Kevin Hasson, "Public Faith," *American Enterprise*, May 2006.

Caroline Hendrie, "Justices Accept Two Cases on Ten Commandments," *Education Week*, October 20, 2004.

K. Hollyn Hollman, "Quiet Case May Have Far-Reaching Impact," *Liberty*, March/April 2006.

James Lawlor, "Wisconsin City Burdens Religious Exercise," *Planning*, May 2005.

Douglas Laycock, "Religious Liberty in America," *Human Rights*, Summer 2006.

Jeremy Leaming, "Invitation to Tea," *Church & State*, April 2006.

———, "Pentacle Quest: Americans United Brings Legal Action to Halt Discrimination Against Wiccans by Veterans Administration," *Church & State*, December 2006.

Adam Liptak, "The First Amendment," *New York Times Upfront*, October 9, 2006.

Robert T. Miller, "Religion Uniquely Disfavored," *First Things*, June 1, 2004.

Vincent Phillip Muñoz, "Establishing Free Exercise," *First Things*, December 2003.

———, "George Washington on Religious Liberty," *Review of Politics*, Winter 2003.

H. Jefferson Powell, "Should Creed or Constitution Guide the Judiciary?" *USA Today*, March 2004.

Stephen B. Presser, "The Ten Commandments Mish-Mosh," *American Spectator*, October 2005.

Warren Richie, "On Docket: Religious Freedom vs. Drug Laws," *Christian Science Monitor*, October 31, 2005.

———, "Supreme Court Will Revisit Issue of Free Exercise of Religion," *Christian Science Monitor*, April 19, 2005.

Mindy Sink, "Peyote, Indian Religion and the Issue of Exclusivity," *New York Times*, August 14, 2004.

Gary Taylor and Helen Hawley, "Freedom of Religion in America," *Contemporary Review*, June 2003.

Internet Sources

American Humanist Association. Amicus curiae brief to the Supreme Court in the pledge of allegiance case, February 12, 2004. www.americanhumanist.org/pledgebrief.pdf.

Alan Keyes, "On the Establishment of Religion: What the Constitution Really Says," RenewAmerica, August 26, 2003. www.renewamerica.us/readings/keyes.pdf.

Elizabeth Ann Massopust and Nathaniel Zylstra, "Religious Freedom and the War on Terror," American Experiment Quarterly, Spring 2004. www.americanexperiment.org/uploaded/files/aeqv7n1massopustzylstra.pdf.

National Association of Evangelicals, "Religious Freedom for Soldiers and Military Chaplains," February 7, 2006. www.mca-usa.org/NAEStatement.pdf.

Jeremiah H. Russell, "The Religious Liberty Argument for Same-Sex Marriage and Its Effect upon Legal Recognition," *Rutgers Journal of Law and Religion*, Vol. 7, December 15, 2005. http://org.law.rutgers.edu/publications/law-religion/articles/7_1_4.pdf.

Index

A

Accommodations for religion
- are not required, 182–183
- compelling governmental interest can override, 152
- establishment clause and, 110
- examples, 113–114, 125–126
- limits to, 53–54, 129
- must be meaningfully enforced, 184

Actions. *See* Conduct
Alito, Samuel, 170
American Civil Liberties Union (ACLU), 59, 131
Americans United for Separation of Church and State, 131
Amish
- education, 20–21, 23–25, 29, 173–174
- rights of children, 33
- taxes, 53–54, 151–152
- traffic laws, 48–49

Amos, 113, 115
Animal sacrifice
- as cruelty to animals and danger to public health, 59, 65, 71
- methods, 97
- religious tradition of, 58
- in Santeria, 62–63

Aryan Nation, 105, 130
Asatru, 105, 129
Ayahuasca use. *See* Hoasca use

B

Baker, Jeanne, 93
Ball, William, 49, 50–51
Banisteriopsis caapi, 147
Barnette, Board of Education v., 35
Barnhart, Linda, 17
Barnhart, William, 17
Barnhart v. Commonwealth of Pennsylvania (1985), 17, 18
Becker Fund for Religious Liberty, 131
Berg, Thomas, 184
Bigamy, 94, 172–173
Blackmun, Harry, 74, 102
Board of Education v. Barnette, 35
Boerne v. Flores, City of, 111, 131, 137, 175–178
Braunfeld v. Brown, 152, 153
Bronfman, Jeffrey, 163, 165
Burger, Warren, 22, 53–54
Bybee, Jay S., 49

C

Caldor, 115
Cardoso, Silvio, 70
Carper, James, 51
Catholicism, 58, 62
Chafetz, Josh, 37
Children
- animal sacrifice harms, 65
- constitutionally protectible interests of, 34–35
- education, 20–21, 23, 25, 35–36, 173–174
- importance of health of, 16, 17
- religious beliefs of, 30, 33, 38

Christian fundamentalist schools, 50–51
Christian Spiritist sect, 143–145
Church of Jesus Christ Christian, 105, 130

Church of Lukumi Babalu Aye v. City of Hialeah (1993)
  arguments of defendant, 91–96
  arguments of petitioner, 96–97
  concurring opinion, 75–77
  decision, 100–101
  majority opinion, 61–73
  overview of, 58–60
City of Boerne v. Flores, 111, 131, 137, 175–178
City of Hialeah, Church of Lukumi Babalu Aye v. (1993). *See Church of Lukumi Babalu Aye v. City of Hialeah* (1993)
City of Indianapolis v. Edmond, 158
Clement, Paul D., 156
Clergy, 134, 135
Commentary on the Constitution (Story), 120
Commonwealth of Massachusetts, Prince v. (1944), 16–17
Commonwealth of Pennsylvania, Barnhart v. (1985), 17, 18
Communitarian theory, 39–46
Compelling governmental interest
  application, 115, 153, 178–180
  balancing with religious liberty, 21, 53–56, 152, 184
  burden of proof for, 172, 173, 177
  in controlling hallucinogens, 147–148
  education, 25, 28
  general applicability principle and, 66, 82–83, 99–100, 169
  intent of law and, 174
  least-restrictive means standard and, 75–76, 83, 84, 184
  neutrality principle and, 66, 82–83, 99–100
  in preventing cruelty to animals, 59
  in protecting public health and safety, 59, 65, 84–85, 91–92, 112, 143, 148, 158
  in social reproduction, 38, 39
  in uniform enforcement, 160–161
Compulsory education laws, 20–21, 23, 25, 173–174
Conduct
  basis of beliefs for, 26
  First Amendment protection and, 27
  government bans must cover all reasons for equivalent, 59
  is part of religious practices, 114
  See also Religious practices
Conservative Amish Mennonite Church, 23
Controlled Substances Act (CSA, 1970)
  closed system established by, 183
  exemptions, 144, 150–151, 159
  marijuana for medical use, 168
  purpose, 157
  Schedule I drugs, 147, 149
Courts
  application of compelling governmental interest test by, 178–180
  rigorousness of standards in cases, 55
  role of, 15
  types of cases, 14–15
Creationism, teaching of, 43–45
Cruelty to animals
  compelling governmental interest in preventing, 59, 71
  general applicability and, 85–86

laws prohibiting, 63–64
methods of sacrifice, 65, 97
preventing in legitimate manner, 69

Cruz, R. Ted, 99

Cutter, Jon B., 138

Cutter et al. v. Wilkinson, Director, Ohio Department of Correction, et al. (2005)
background of, 124, 139
concurring opinion, 117–122, 132
establishment clause and, 153, 178
overview of, 105–107
unanimous opinion, 109–116, 129, 132

D

Davey, Locke v., 110

Democratic-communitarian theory, 39–46

Des Moines School District, Tinker v., 34–35

Dimethyltryptamine (DMT), 163
in hoasca, 147, 148
increase in use, 165
in peyote, 169
potential for abuse, 159
Schedule I drug, 149, 157
See also Hoasca use

Dissent, suppression of, 45

Dissent, tradition of, 46

Dorf, Michael C., 171

Dornan, Bob, 52

Douglas, William O., 32

Drinan, Robert F., 78

Drugs
abuse of, 157, 158, 159
marijuana, 168, 177
See also Hallucinogens; Hoasca use

Due process clause, 100, 102, 175

E

Echevarria, Herman, 70

Eckstrom, Keith, 167

Edmond, City of Indianapolis v., 158

Education
Amish and, 23–25, 29
Christian fundamentalist schools, 50–51
compulsory, 20–21, 23, 25, 173–174
curriculum decisions, 43–45
is not value-neutral, 40
minors' views, 35–36
not government function in early republic, 38
outside of schools, 45
separate school districts, 115
way of life and, 28, 38, 39, 41–42
Wisconsin v. Yoder as precedent setter, 49–52

Eilers, Dana D., 136

Elk Grove Unified School Dist. v. Newdow, 118

Employment
of children, 16–17
eligibility for unemployment benefits, 49, 55, 76, 152, 173
religious practices and, 81–82, 110–111
on Sabbath, 115, 172, 173, 177
Social Security taxes and, 53–54, 151–152

Employment Div., Dept. of Human Resources of Ore. v. Smith (1990)
background of, 81
concurring opinion, 77

decision, 99–100, 114, 137
dissenting opinion, 75
effect, 21, 54–56, 84, 143
legislative responses, 106
majority opinion, 55, 81–82, 131, 174, 180
as precedent, 88, 102
RLUIPA and, 110–111
Equal protection clause, 100, 102
Erickson, Donald, 29
Establishment clause
accommodations for religion and, 110, 115
Constitution framers and, 118–120
court cases, 14
legislation, 178
protects state governments from federal government, 118, 121, 132
separation of church and state, 113
Evolution, teaching of, 43–45

F

Faith healing, 16, 17
Faith Tabernacle Church, 17
Federal government
First Amendment limits on, 14, 118, 121, 132
Fourteenth Amendment limits on, 111
funds to states, 122, 132, 134, 140
involvement in medicine, 18
neutrality requirement, 27–28
RFRA applied to, 176
tax system, 53–54, 151–152
unique relationship with Native American tribes, 162
Federalism, 14, 111, 117–118, 132
First Amendment
limits on federal government, 14, 118, 121, 132
religious practices and, 27, 83–84
wording, 113
Flags, saluting, 35
Flores, City of Boerne v., 111, 131, 137, 175–178
Florida, Hobbie v. Unemployment Appeals Comm'n of, 110
Formal equality principle, 174
Fourteenth Amendment
limits on federal government, 111
limits on state governments, 14, 38
RFRA and, 175
Free exercise clause
court cases, 14–15
due process clause, 175
equal protection, 100, 102
formal equality principle, 174
general applicability principle, 70–71
importance of, to minority religions, 86
in military community, 114
noninterference with religious beliefs and practices, 113
religiously grounded conduct and government police power, 27
Freeze v. Illinois Dept. of Employment Security (1989), 66

G

Garnett, Richard, 181
Garrett, Richard, 91–96
General applicability principle
burden of proof, 173–174
compelling governmental interest and, 66, 82–83, 99–100

- does not usually allow burdening of exercise of religion, 184
- exemptions, 169, 173
- free exercise clause and, 70–71
- importance of, vs. religious practices, is legislative function, 178–179
- neutrality principle and, 88–90
- to non-religious practices, 85–86
- police power of government, 27

Ginsberg, Ruth Bader, 108, 129, 132

Goldberger, David, 129–131, 133

Goldman v. Weinberger, 114

Gonzales, Attorney General, et al. v. O Centro Espirita Beneficiente Uniao de Vegetal, et al. (2006)
- brief for petitioners, 157–166
- overview of, 143–145
- unanimous opinion, 147–155, 168, 169, 170, 178–179, 182, 183–184

Gonzales v. Raich, 177

Gorman, Peter, 144

Guided evolution, teaching of, 43–45

H

Hallucinogens
- damage health, 163–164
- government has compelling interest in controlling, 147–148
- increase in use, 157, 161, 166
- peyote use by Native Americans, 81–82, 110–111, 143, 144, 150, 169
- *See also* Hoasca use

Hamburger, Philip, 118

Hamilton, Mitzi, 127–128, 133–134

Hampton, J. Lee, 138

Harmelin v. Michigan, 158

Hasidim, 115

Haynes, Charles C., 123, 168

Health, 16, 17
- *See also* Public health and safety

Hernandez, 153

Herrera, C.D., 18

Hialeah, Church of Lukumi Babalu Aye v. City of (1993). *See Church of Lukumi Babalu Aye v. City of Hialeah* (1993)

Hoasca use
- abuse, 159, 160, 166
- is health risk, 148, 163–164
- as religious practice, 143–145, 147, 182
- UN Convention on Psychotropic Substances and, 154

Hobbie v. Unemployment Appeals Comm'n of Fla., 110

Home schooling, 49, 51–52

Huffman, Jennifer L., 78

I

Illegal drugs
- abuse of, 157, 158, 159
- marijuana, 168, 177
- *See also* Hallucinogens; Hoasca use

Illinois Dept. of Employment Security, Freeze v. (1989), 66

Indiana Employment Security Div., Thomas v. Review Bd. of (1981), 66, 75–76

Indianapolis v. Edmond, City of, 158

Institutions. *See Cutter et al. v. Wilkinson, Director, Ohio Department of Correction, et al.* (2005)
Intent (of laws)
  achievement methods, 75–76
  animus in, 45–46
  compelling governmental interest and, 174
  suppression of minority religions, 66–73, 76–77, 84
Iredell, James, 119
Islam, 134, 135

J

Jefferson, Thomas, 28, 29–30
Journal of Church and State, 18
Judaism, 115, 127–128, 133–135

K

Kennedy, Arthur, 61, 93–95, 175
Kiryas Joel, 115

L

Laycock, David, 88–91, 96–97
Leaming, Jeremy, 127
Learning-by-doing education, 29
Least-restrictive means standard
  compelling governmental interest and, 75–76, 83, 84, 184
  in RFRA, 82–83
Lee, Edwin, 53
Lee, United States v., 53–54, 151–152, 153
Leland, Jared, 168
Local governments. *See* State governments
Locke, John, 101
Locke v. Davey, 110
Lukumi Babalu Aye Church. *See Church of Lukumi Babalu Aye v. City of Hialeah* (1993)
Lukumi (religion), 58
Lukumi v. Hialeah. See Church of Lukumi Babalu Aye v. City of Hialeah (1993)
Lynn, Barry W., 125, 133

M

Madison, James, 119
Marijuana for medical use, 168, 177
Massachusetts, Prince v. Commonwealth of (1944), 16–17
McConnell, Michael, 162
McDaniel v. Paty, 72
McFarland, Steven, 98
McKewen, Richard, 128, 133–134
Medicine/medical treatment
  government involvement in, 18
  marijuana as, 168, 177
  rejection of, 16, 17–18
Mejides, Andres, 70
Meyer v. Nebraska (1923), 52
Michigan, Harmelin v., 158
Military, 114
Miller, Barbara, 34
Miller, Wallace, 20–21, 23, 34
Minority religions
  formal equality principle, 174
  free exercise clause, 86
  neutrality principle as test of burden on, 131
  protecting, in political process, 178
  supporting rights of each other, 82

suppressing, as intent of law, 66–73, 76–77, 84
See also specific religions; specific sects
Mormon Church, 94, 172–173
Murray, John Courtney, 185

N

National Association of Evangelicals, 168
National Committee for Amish Religious Freedom (NCARF), 20–21
National Treasury Employees Union v. Von Raab, 158
Native Americans
peyote use, 81–82, 110–111, 143, 144, 150, 169
unique relationship between tribes and federal government, 162
Nebraska, Meyer v. (1923), 52
Neutrality principle
compelling governmental interest and, 66, 82–83, 99–100
education does not meet, 40
established as standard, 55
general applicability principle and, 88–90
may burden religious practices, 154
RLUIPA and, 141
suspect circumstances, 69–70
target of law, 92
as test for burdening minority religions, 131
underlies guarantee of freedom of religion, 17
undue burden and, 27–28
Newdow, Elk Grove Unified School Dist. v., 118
Non-mainstream religions. *See* Minority religions

O

O Centro Espirita Beneficiente Uniao de Vegetal, et al., Gonzales, Attorney General, et al. v. (2006). *See Gonzales, Attorney General, et al. v. O Centro Espirita Beneficiente Uniao de Vegetal, et al.* (2006)
O'Brien, David M., 87
O'Connor, Sandra Day, 92, 93
Ohio Department of Correction, et al., Cutter et al. v. Wilkinson, Director. See Cutter et al. v. Wilkinson, Director Ohio Department of Corrections, et al. (2005)
Old Order Amish
education and, 20–21, 23–25, 29
rights of children, 33
Oregon v. Smith, Employment Div., Dept. of Human Resources of (1990). *See Employment Div., Dept. of Human Resources of Ore. v. Smith* (1990)
Orishas, 58, 62, 80
Overinclusivity of law, 75–76

P

Paganism, 136
Parens patriae (guardian of all minors), 30
Parental rights
acting contrary to best interests of children, 31, 33
education and, 20–21
government as *parens patriae* and, 30
home schooling, 51–52
medical care of children, 16, 17

as only source of values for children, 40
See also Wisconsin v. Yoder (1972)
Parental Rights and Responsibilities bill (1995), 52
Paty, McDaniel v., 72
Pennsylvania, Barnhart v. Commonwealth of (1985), 17, 18
Peters, Shawn Francis, 48
Peyote use by Native Americans, 81–82, 110–111, 143, 144, 150, 169
Picarello, Anthony, 125
Pichardo, Ernesto, 58–59, 64, 80, 100
Pierce v. Society of Sisters (1925), 25, 52
Polygamy, 94, 172–173
Prayer in public schools, 14
Precedents (legal)
importance of, 15, 88
Smith as, 88, 102
use of, 77
Yoder as, 49–52
Prince, Sarah, 16–17
Prince v. Commonwealth of Massachusetts (1944), 16–17
Prison Litigation Reform Act (1995), 116
Prisons
barriers to religious practices in, 105, 109, 111–112
compelling governmental interest in security, 112
See also Cutter et al. v. Wilkinson, Director, Ohio Department of Correction, et al. (2005)
Psychotria viridis, 147
Public health and safety
animal killings as risk to, 65, 71
compelling governmental interest in protecting, 59, 65, 84–85, 91–92, 112, 143, 148, 158
consumption of uninspected meat as risk to, 72
controlled substances damage, regardless of users' motivation, 159
hoasca use harms, 163–164
marijuana as medicine, 168, 177
protecting in legitimate manner, 68–69
Public schools
head coverings in, 126
prayer in, 14
separate school districts, 115
See also Education
Pullman, Sarah, 167

R

Rabinove, Sam, 98
Raich, Gonzales v., 177
Rehnquist, William, 89, 90–91, 92
Religious beliefs
of children, 30, 33, 38
compelling governmental interest and, 53–56
free exercise clause noninterference with, 113
practices required by, 79–80, 81, 182
protection of nature of, 65–66
religious practices vs., 83–84, 101
sincerity of, 106, 138
as source of legal exemptions, 46
way of life and, 26, 27
Religious Freedom Restoration Act (RFRA, 1993)
declared unconstitutional, 137, 175

effect, 106
establishment clause, 178
least-restrictive means standard, 82–83
provisions, 111, 168
purpose, 55–56, 143, 174, 183
separation of powers and, 178–179
upheld as applied to federal government, 176

Religious Land Use and Institutionalized Persons Act (RLUIPA, 2000)
background of, 110–112
establishment clause, 178
neutrality principle, 141
provisions, 106, 109, 125

Religious practices
accommodations for, are not required, 182–183
barriers to, in institutions, 105, 109, 111–112, 127–128, 133–135
can be unconstitutional, 94
central to beliefs, 79–80, 81, 114, 182
employment and, 81–82, 110–111
First Amendment protection and, 27
free exercise clause noninterference with, 113
government decision as to necessity, 88
government may interfere with, 72–73, 76–77, 173
importance of, vs. general applicability principle is legislative function, 178–179
neutrality principle may burden, 154
religious beliefs vs., 83–84, 101
removal of government-imposed burdens is accommodation, 113–114
Sabbath observance, 152
wearing specific items, 114, 126

Review Bd. of Indiana Employment Security Div., Thomas v. (1981), 66

Reynolds, George, 172–173

Reynolds v. United States (1878), 94, 173, 174

Roberts, John, 146, 168, 169, 170, 178–179, 182, 183–184

Roman Catholicism, 58, 62

Rutledge, Wiley, 17

S

Santeria, 58, 62–63, 79–80, 83, 100–101

Santo Daime Church, 160

Satanism, 105, 130

Satmar Hasidim, 115

Scalia, Antonin
in *Church of Lukumi Babalu Aye,* 89–90, 96, 97
in *Smith,* 55, 81–82, 131, 174, 178, 180

Schedule I drugs, 147, 149, 150

Separation of church and state
defining elements of, 185
establishment clause and, 113
public opinion about, 14

Separation of powers, 178–179

Seventh Day Adventists, 173

Shackelford, Kelly, 169

Sherbert v. Verner (1963), 49, 55, 76, 152, 173

Slippery-slope argument, 152

Smith, Employment Division v. (1990). *See Employment Div., Dept. of Human Resources of Ore. v. Smith* (1990)
Social reproduction, 38, 39
Social Security taxes, 53–54, 151–152
Society of Sisters, Pierce v. (1925), 25, 52
Souter, David, 88, 90
Speech, freedom of, 34–35
Spiritist sect, 143–145
State governments
  Congressional power over laws of, 175–176
  establishment clause protects, from federal government, 118, 121, 132
  Fourteenth Amendment limits on, 14, 38
  funds from federal government, 122, 132, 134, 140
  involvement in medicine, 18
  medical rights of, 177
  as *parens patriae,* 30
Stevens, John Paul, 95, 176–178
Story, Joseph, 120
Sunday closing laws, 152
Swan, Rita, 16

T

Tabernacle Christian School, 50–51
Textbooks, 49
Thomas, Clarence, 117, 132
Thomas v. Review Bd. of Indiana Employment Security Div. (1981), 66, 75–76
Thoreau, Henry David, 26
Tinker v. Des Moines School District, 34–35
Totalitarianism, 39, 45
Traffic laws and Amish, 48–49

U

Underinclusivity of law, 71, 75–76
Unemployment Appeals Comm'n of Fla., Hobbie v., 110
Uniform enforcement principle, 151–152, 160–161, 184
United Nations Convention on Psychotropic Substances (1971), 153–154
United States, Reynolds v., 94, 173, 174
U.S. Constitution. *See* First Amendment; Fourteenth Amendment
U.S. Constitution ratification debates, 119
United States v. Lee, 53–54, 151–152, 153

V

Verner, Sherbert v. (1963), 49, 55, 76, 152, 173
Von Raab, National Treasury Employees Union v., 158

W

Way of life and education, 28, 38, 39, 41–42
Way of life and religious beliefs, 26, 27
Weinberger, Goldman v., 114
Whisner, Levi W., 50–51
White supremacist organizations, 105, 130
Wicca, 105, 130
Wilkinson, Director, Ohio Department of Correction, et al., Cutter et al. v. (2005). *See Cutter et al. v. Wilkinson, Director, Ohio Department of Correction, et al.* (2005)

Wisconsin v. Yoder (1972)
decision, 173–174
decision as anti-democratic, 41, 42–43
dissenting opinion, 33–36
effect of, 75–76
majority opinion, 23–31
overturned, 21, 54–56
overview of, 20–21
as precedent setter, 49–52

Y

Yoder, Frieda, 34
Yoder, Jonas, 20–21, 23, 34
Yoder, Wisconsin v. (1972). *See Wisconsin v. Yoder* (1972)
Yoruba, 58, 62–63, 79–80, 83, 100–101
Yutzy, Adin, 20–21, 23, 34
Yutzy, Vernon, 34